HARCOURT

Math

Teacher's Resource Book

Grade 4

Harcourt

Orlando   Austin   Chicago   New York   Toronto   London   San Diego

Visit *The Learning Site!*
www.harcourtschool.com

ISBN 0-15-336866-7

6 7 8 9 10   073   10 09 08 07 06 05

CONTENTS

PROBLEM SOLVING

NUMBER AND OPERATIONS

TIME, MONEY, MEASUREMENT

GEOMETRY

DATA, PROBABILITY, AND GRAPHING

TEACHER'S EDITION PRACTICE GAMES

DAILY FACTS PRACTICE

FACT CARDS

VOCABULARY CARDS

IT'S IN THE BAG

Problem Solving

Understand

1. Retell the problem in your own words. _____

_____

_____

_____

2. List the information given. _____

_____

3. Restate the question as a fill-in-the-blank sentence. _____

_____

Plan

4. List one or more problem-solving strategies that you can use. _____

_____

5. Predict what your answer will be. _____

_____

Solve

6. Show how you solved the problem. _____

_____

_____

_____

7. Write your answer in a complete sentence. _____

_____

Check

8. Tell how you know your answer is reasonable. _____

_____

9. Describe another way you could have solved the problem. _____

_____

Problem Solving Think Along

Understand

1. What is the problem about?

2. What information is given in the problem?

3. What is the question?

Plan

4. What problem-solving strategies might I try to help me solve the problem?

5. About what do I think my answer will be?

Solve

6. How can I solve the problem?

7. How can I state my answer in a complete sentence?

Check

8. How do I know whether my answer is reasonable?

9. How else might I have solved this problem?

4

0

5

1

6

2

7

3

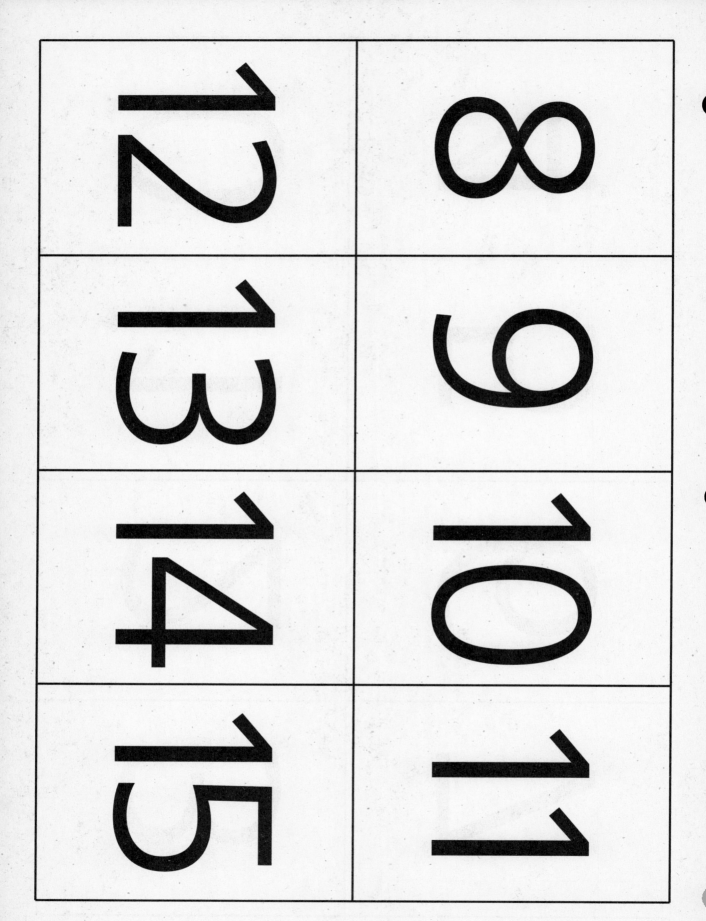

Number line 0 to 22:

0 1 2 3 4 5 6 7 8 9 10 11 12 13 14 15 16 17 18 19 20 21 22

Number line 20 to 42:

20 21 22 23 24 25 26 27 28 29 30 31 32 33 34 35 36 37 38 39 40 41 42

Number line 40 to 62:

40 41 42 43 44 45 46 47 48 49 50 51 52 53 54 55 56 57 58 59 60 61 62

Number line 60 to 82:

60 61 62 63 64 65 66 67 68 69 70 71 72 73 74 75 76 77 78 79 80 81 82

Number line 80 to 102:

80 81 82 83 84 85 86 87 88 89 90 91 92 93 94 95 96 97 98 99 100 101 102

Number Lines

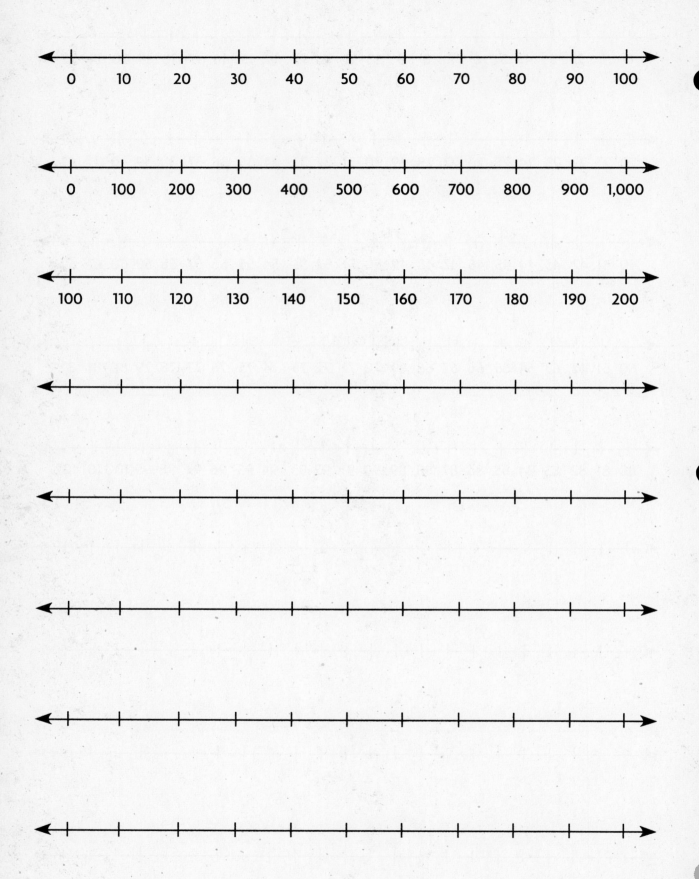

Number lines:

0 +1 +2 +3 +4 +5 +6 +7 +8 +9 +10 +11 +12 +13 +14 +15 +16 +17 +18 +19 +20

-20 -19 -18 -17 -16 -15 -14 -13 -12 -11 -10 -9 -8 -7 -6 -5 -4 -3 -2 -1 0

-10 -9 -8 -7 -6 -5 -4 -3 -2 -1 0 +1 +2 +3 +4 +5 +6 +7 +8 +9 +10

-10 -9 -8 -7 -6 -5 -4 -3 -2 -1 0 +1 +2 +3 +4 +5 +6 +7 +8 +9 +10

Number Lines

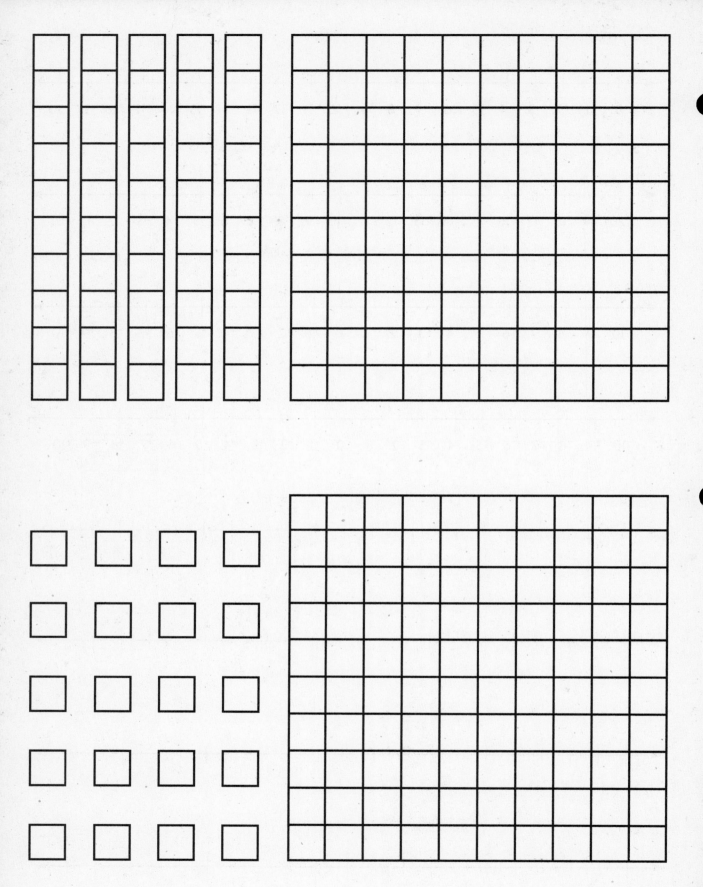

Base-Ten Materials

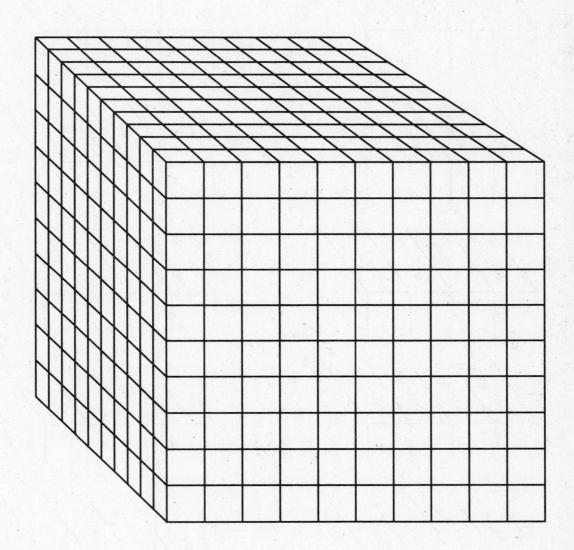

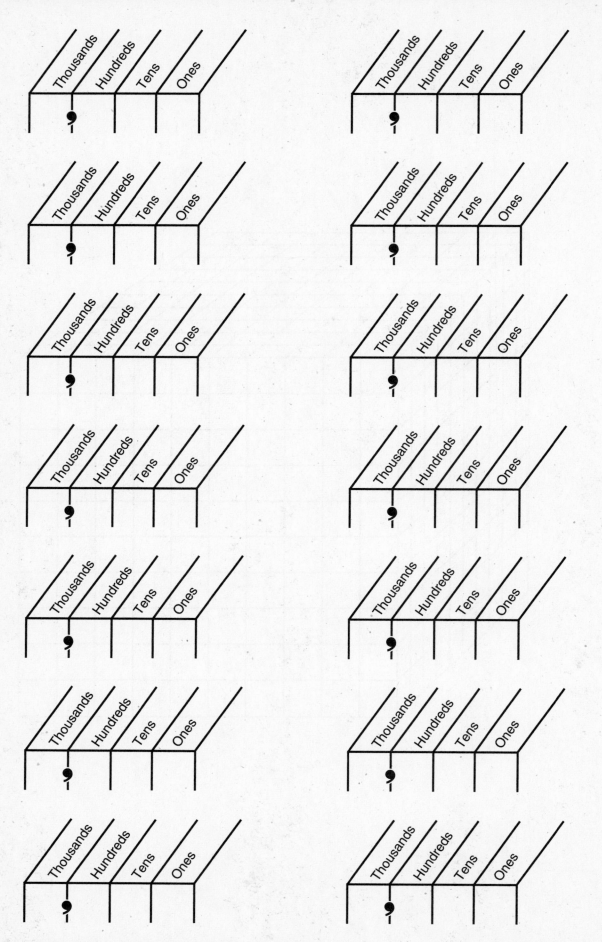

Place-Value Charts

Place-value chart headers (each of 14 charts): Hundred Thousands | Ten Thousands | Thousands | Hundreds | Tens | Ones

© Harcourt

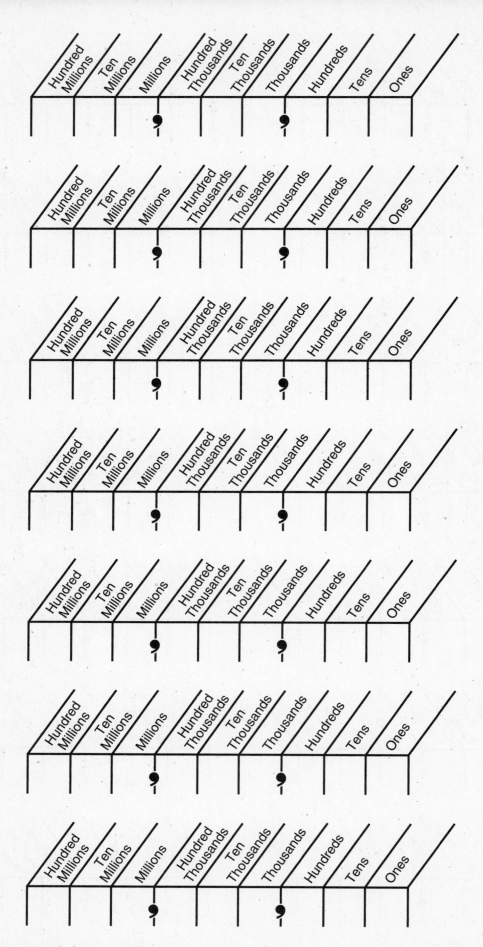

Place-Value Charts

Ones	Tens	Hundreds	Thousands

Millions	Hundred Thousands	Ten Thousands	Thousands	Hundreds	Tens	Ones

	0	1	2	3	4	5	6	7	8	9	10	11	12
0													
1													
2													
3													
4													
5													
6													
7													
8													
9													
10													
11													
12													

Addition/Multiplication Table

×	1	2	3	4	5	6	7	8	9	10	11	12
1	1	2	3	4	5	6	7	8	9	10	11	12
2	2	4	6	8	10	12	14	16	18	20	22	24
3	3	6	9	12	15	18	21	24	27	30	33	36
4	4	8	12	16	20	24	28	32	36	40	44	48
5	5	10	15	20	25	30	35	40	45	50	55	60
6	6	12	18	24	30	36	42	48	54	60	66	72
7	7	14	21	28	35	42	49	56	63	70	77	84
8	8	16	24	32	40	48	56	64	72	80	88	96
9	9	18	27	36	45	54	63	72	81	90	99	108
10	10	20	30	40	50	60	70	80	90	100	110	120
11	11	22	33	44	55	66	77	88	99	110	121	132
12	12	24	36	48	60	72	84	96	108	120	132	144

Multiplication Table

3 × 3 Grids

| $\frac{1}{12}$ | $\frac{1}{12}$ | $\frac{1}{12}$ | $\frac{1}{12}$ | $\frac{1}{12}$ | $\frac{1}{12}$ | $\frac{1}{12}$ | $\frac{1}{12}$ | $\frac{1}{12}$ | $\frac{1}{12}$ | $\frac{1}{12}$ | $\frac{1}{12}$ |

| $\frac{1}{11}$ | $\frac{1}{11}$ | $\frac{1}{11}$ | $\frac{1}{11}$ | $\frac{1}{11}$ | $\frac{1}{11}$ | $\frac{1}{11}$ | $\frac{1}{11}$ | $\frac{1}{11}$ | $\frac{1}{11}$ | $\frac{1}{11}$ |

| $\frac{1}{10}$ | $\frac{1}{10}$ | $\frac{1}{10}$ | $\frac{1}{10}$ | $\frac{1}{10}$ | $\frac{1}{10}$ | $\frac{1}{10}$ | $\frac{1}{10}$ | $\frac{1}{10}$ | $\frac{1}{10}$ |

| $\frac{1}{9}$ | $\frac{1}{9}$ | $\frac{1}{9}$ | $\frac{1}{9}$ | $\frac{1}{9}$ | $\frac{1}{9}$ | $\frac{1}{9}$ | $\frac{1}{9}$ | $\frac{1}{9}$ |

| $\frac{1}{8}$ | $\frac{1}{8}$ | $\frac{1}{8}$ | $\frac{1}{8}$ | $\frac{1}{8}$ | $\frac{1}{8}$ | $\frac{1}{8}$ | $\frac{1}{8}$ |

| $\frac{1}{7}$ | $\frac{1}{7}$ | $\frac{1}{7}$ | $\frac{1}{7}$ | $\frac{1}{7}$ | $\frac{1}{7}$ | $\frac{1}{7}$ |

| $\frac{1}{6}$ | $\frac{1}{6}$ | $\frac{1}{6}$ | $\frac{1}{6}$ | $\frac{1}{6}$ | $\frac{1}{6}$ |

| $\frac{1}{5}$ | $\frac{1}{5}$ | $\frac{1}{5}$ | $\frac{1}{5}$ | $\frac{1}{5}$ |

| $\frac{1}{4}$ | $\frac{1}{4}$ | $\frac{1}{4}$ | $\frac{1}{4}$ |

| $\frac{1}{3}$ | $\frac{1}{3}$ | $\frac{1}{3}$ |

| $\frac{1}{2}$ | $\frac{1}{2}$ |

| 1 |

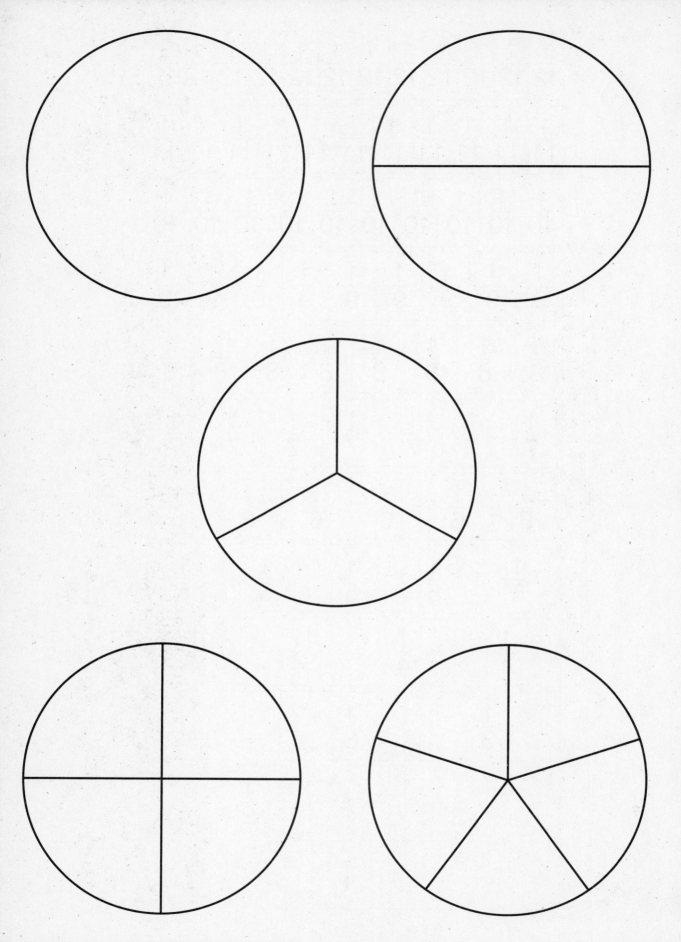

Fraction Circles

Fraction Circles

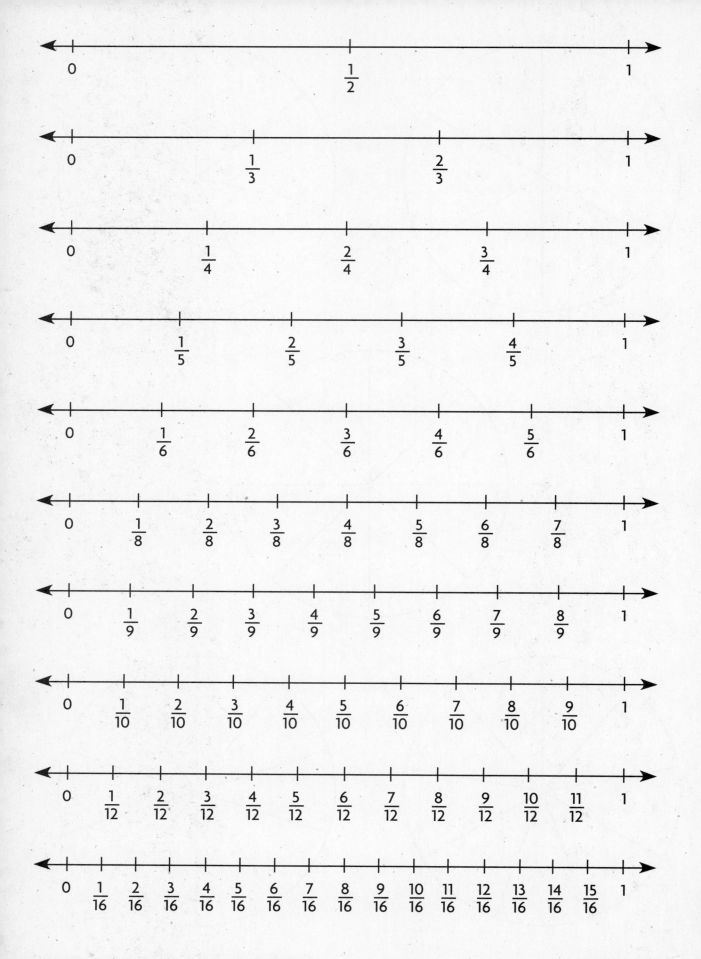

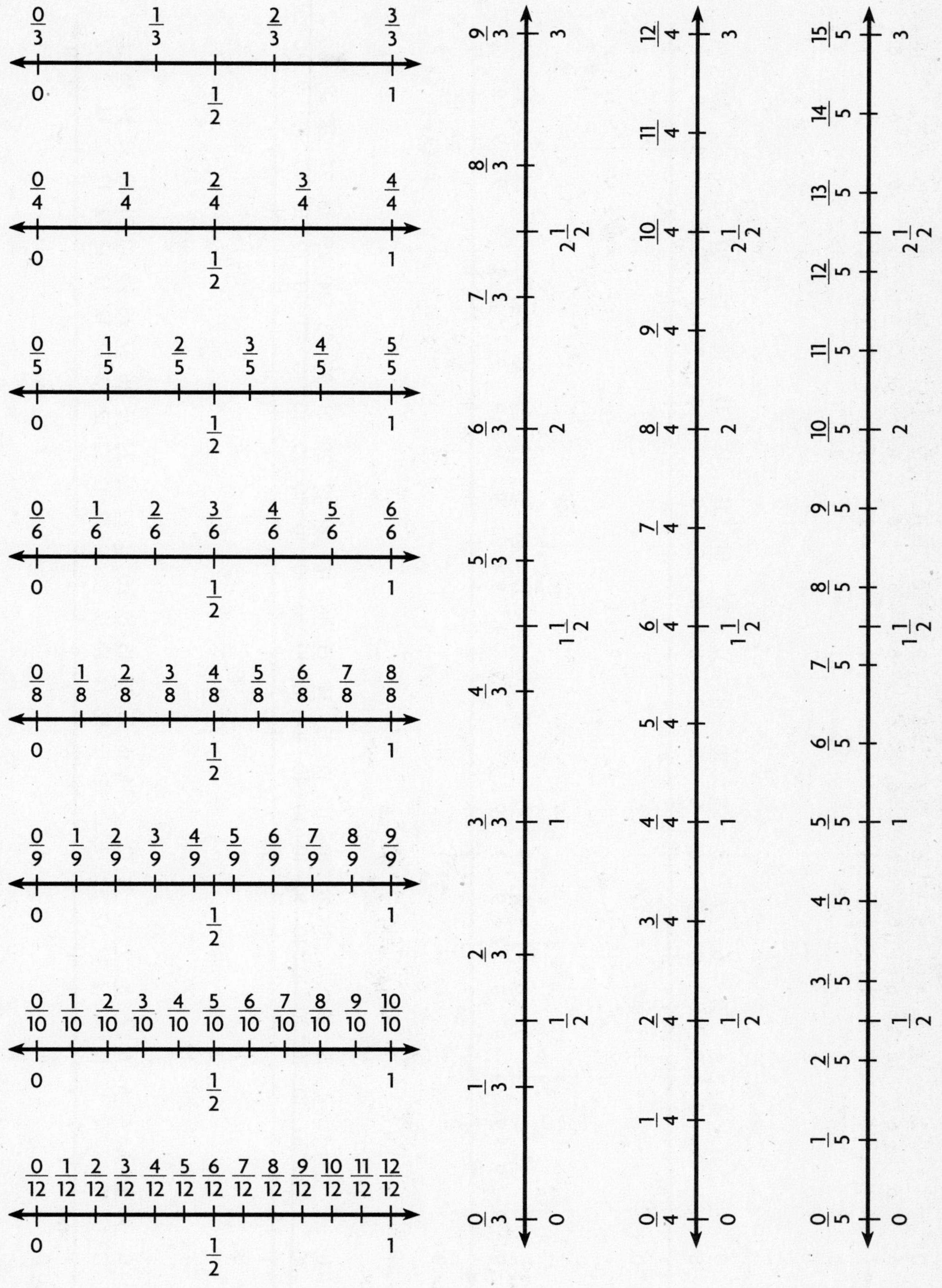

Number lines (thirds):
$\frac{0}{3}$ · $\frac{1}{3}$ · $\frac{2}{3}$ · $\frac{3}{3}$
0 · $\frac{1}{2}$ · 1

Number lines (fourths):
$\frac{0}{4}$ · $\frac{1}{4}$ · $\frac{2}{4}$ · $\frac{3}{4}$ · $\frac{4}{4}$
0 · $\frac{1}{2}$ · 1

Number lines (fifths):
$\frac{0}{5}$ · $\frac{1}{5}$ · $\frac{2}{5}$ · $\frac{3}{5}$ · $\frac{4}{5}$ · $\frac{5}{5}$
0 · $\frac{1}{2}$ · 1

Number lines (sixths):
$\frac{0}{6}$ · $\frac{1}{6}$ · $\frac{2}{6}$ · $\frac{3}{6}$ · $\frac{4}{6}$ · $\frac{5}{6}$ · $\frac{6}{6}$
0 · $\frac{1}{2}$ · 1

Number lines (eighths):
$\frac{0}{8}$ · $\frac{1}{8}$ · $\frac{2}{8}$ · $\frac{3}{8}$ · $\frac{4}{8}$ · $\frac{5}{8}$ · $\frac{6}{8}$ · $\frac{7}{8}$ · $\frac{8}{8}$
0 · $\frac{1}{2}$ · 1

Number lines (ninths):
$\frac{0}{9}$ · $\frac{1}{9}$ · $\frac{2}{9}$ · $\frac{3}{9}$ · $\frac{4}{9}$ · $\frac{5}{9}$ · $\frac{6}{9}$ · $\frac{7}{9}$ · $\frac{8}{9}$ · $\frac{9}{9}$
0 · $\frac{1}{2}$ · 1

Number lines (tenths):
$\frac{0}{10}$ · $\frac{1}{10}$ · $\frac{2}{10}$ · $\frac{3}{10}$ · $\frac{4}{10}$ · $\frac{5}{10}$ · $\frac{6}{10}$ · $\frac{7}{10}$ · $\frac{8}{10}$ · $\frac{9}{10}$ · $\frac{10}{10}$
0 · $\frac{1}{2}$ · 1

Number lines (twelfths):
$\frac{0}{12}$ · $\frac{1}{12}$ · $\frac{2}{12}$ · $\frac{3}{12}$ · $\frac{4}{12}$ · $\frac{5}{12}$ · $\frac{6}{12}$ · $\frac{7}{12}$ · $\frac{8}{12}$ · $\frac{9}{12}$ · $\frac{10}{12}$ · $\frac{11}{12}$ · $\frac{12}{12}$
0 · $\frac{1}{2}$ · 1

Vertical number line (thirds):
$\frac{9}{3}$ — 3
$\frac{8}{3}$
$\frac{7}{3}$ — $2\frac{1}{2}$
$\frac{6}{3}$ — 2
$\frac{5}{3}$
$\frac{4}{3}$ — $1\frac{1}{2}$
$\frac{3}{3}$ — 1
$\frac{2}{3}$
$\frac{1}{3}$ — $\frac{1}{2}$
$\frac{0}{3}$ — 0

Vertical number line (fourths):
$\frac{12}{4}$ — 3
$\frac{11}{4}$
$\frac{10}{4}$ — $2\frac{1}{2}$
$\frac{9}{4}$
$\frac{8}{4}$ — 2
$\frac{7}{4}$
$\frac{6}{4}$ — $1\frac{1}{2}$
$\frac{5}{4}$
$\frac{4}{4}$ — 1
$\frac{3}{4}$
$\frac{2}{4}$ — $\frac{1}{2}$
$\frac{1}{4}$
$\frac{0}{4}$ — 0

Vertical number line (fifths):
$\frac{15}{5}$ — 3
$\frac{14}{5}$
$\frac{13}{5}$
$\frac{12}{5}$ — $2\frac{1}{2}$
$\frac{11}{5}$
$\frac{10}{5}$ — 2
$\frac{9}{5}$
$\frac{8}{5}$
$\frac{7}{5}$ — $1\frac{1}{2}$
$\frac{6}{5}$
$\frac{5}{5}$ — 1
$\frac{4}{5}$
$\frac{3}{5}$
$\frac{2}{5}$ — $\frac{1}{2}$
$\frac{1}{5}$
$\frac{0}{5}$ — 0

Number Lines

© Harcourt

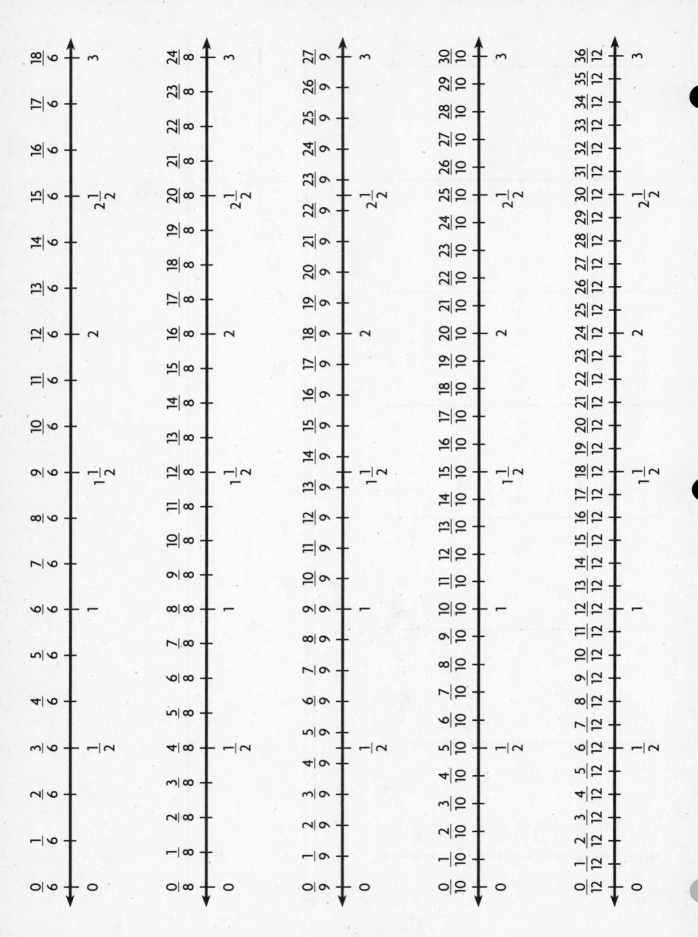

Decimal Models

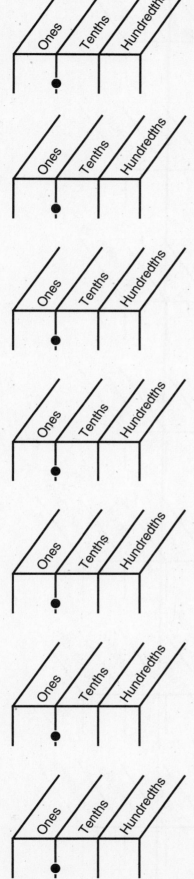
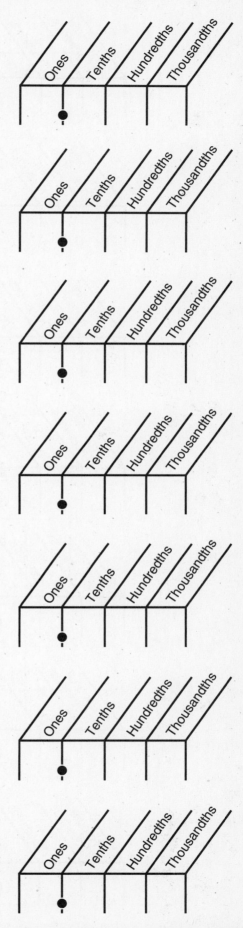

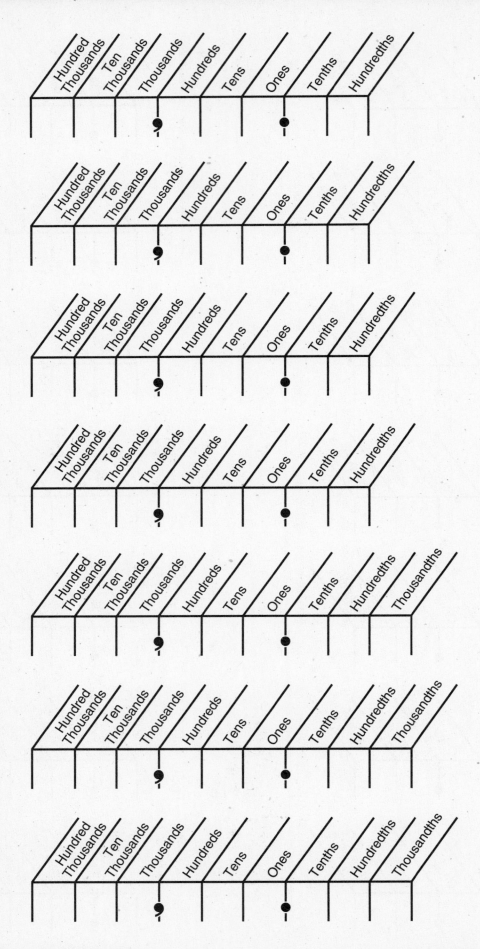

Place-Value Charts

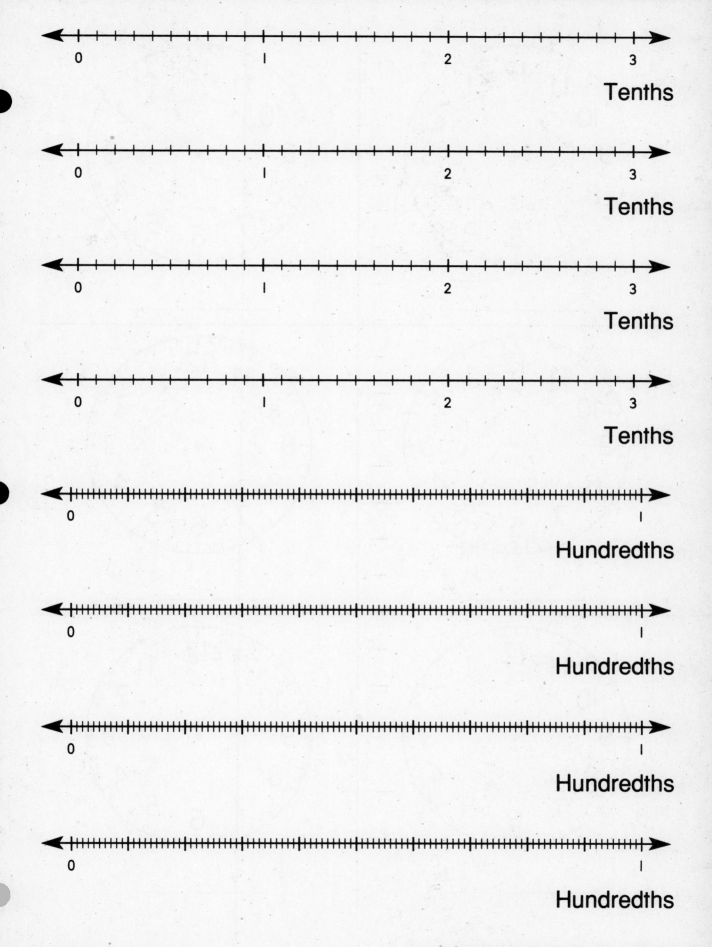

Tenths

Tenths

Tenths

Tenths

Hundredths

Hundredths

Hundredths

Hundredths

© Harcourt

Analog Clockfaces

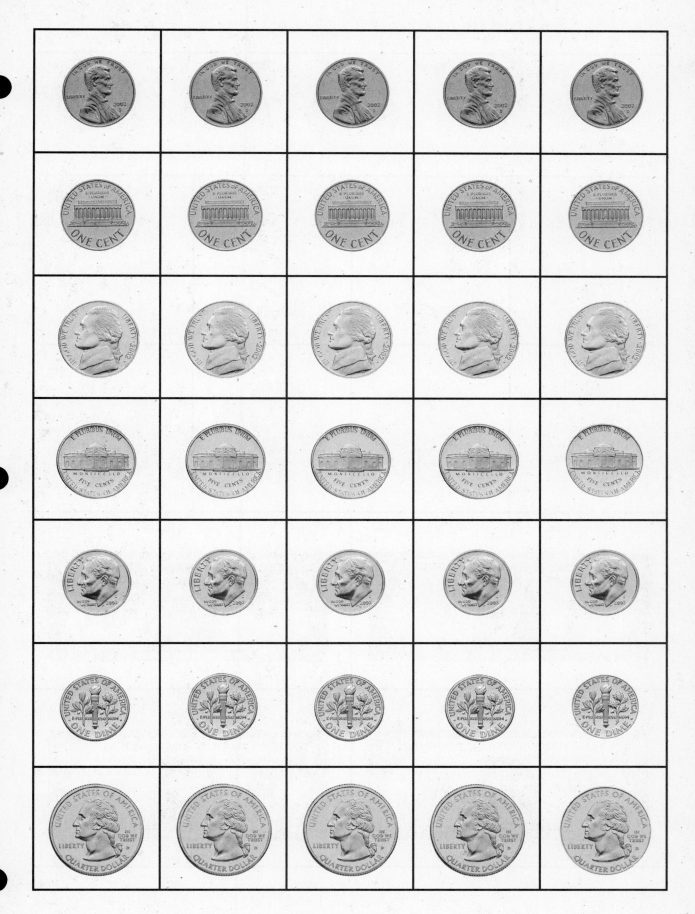

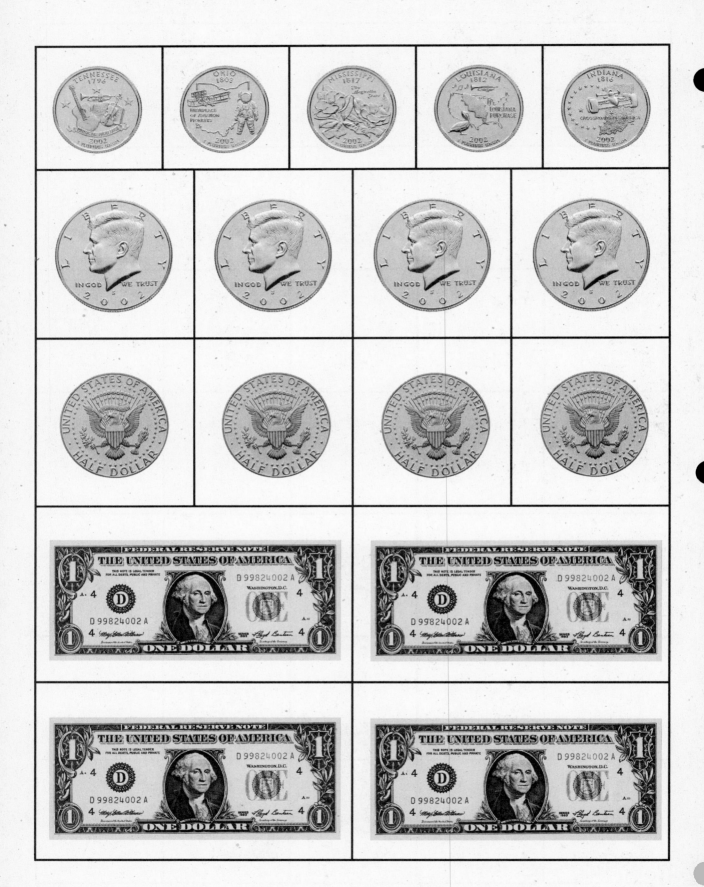

Coins and Bills

Bills

Bills

Sunday	Monday	Tuesday	Wednesday	Thursday	Friday	Saturday

© Harcourt

Blank Calendar

inches

1 2 3 4 5 6 7 8 9

inches

1 2 3 4 5 6 7 8 9

cm
1 2 3 4 5 6 7 8 9 10 11 12 13 14 15 16 17 18 19 20 21 22

1 dm (decimeter) 2 dm

cm
1 2 3 4 5 6 7 8 9 10 11 12 13 14 15 16 17 18 19 20 21 22

1 dm (decimeter) 2 dm

Rulers

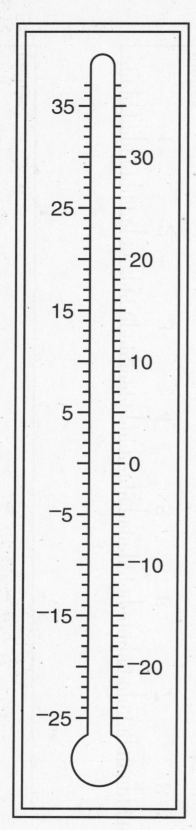

Celsius

_____ °C

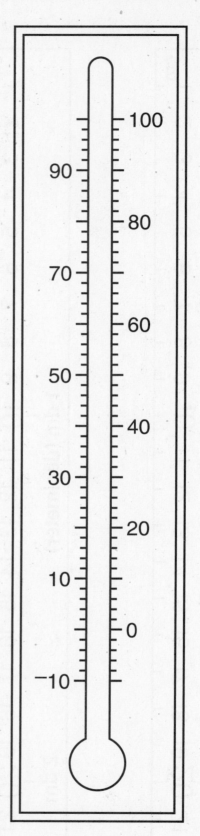

Fahrenheit

_____ °F

Thermometers

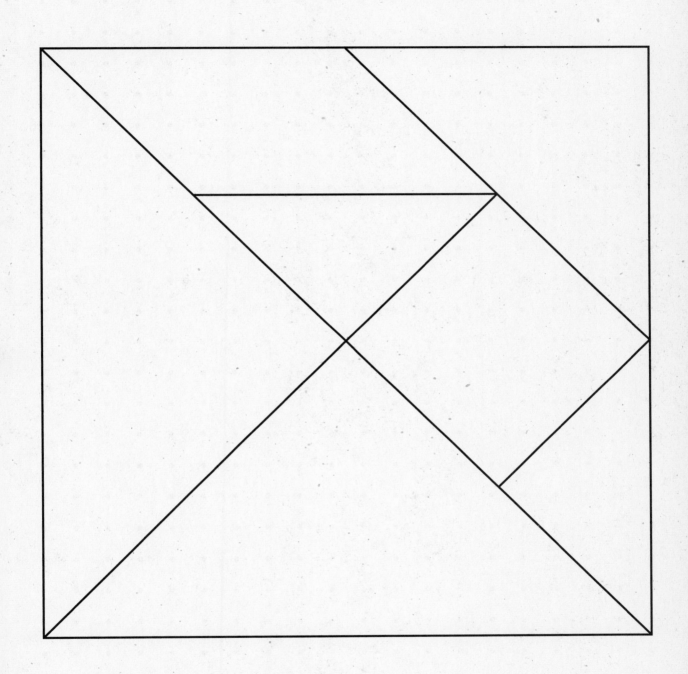

Tangram Pattern

Dot Paper

© Harcourt

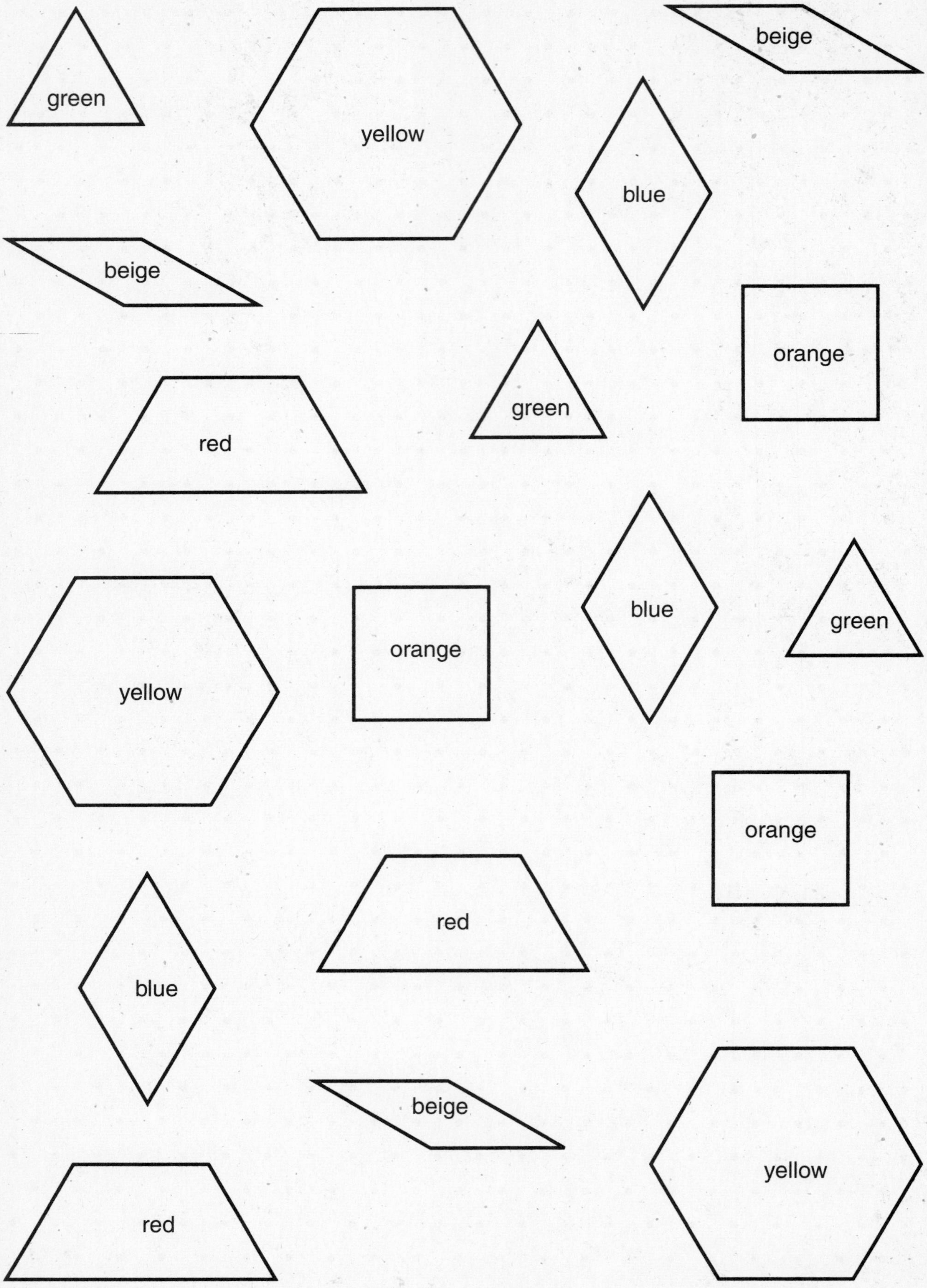

green

yellow

beige

beige

blue

red

green

orange

yellow

orange

blue

green

orange

blue

red

beige

red

yellow

Pattern Block Patterns

© Harcourt

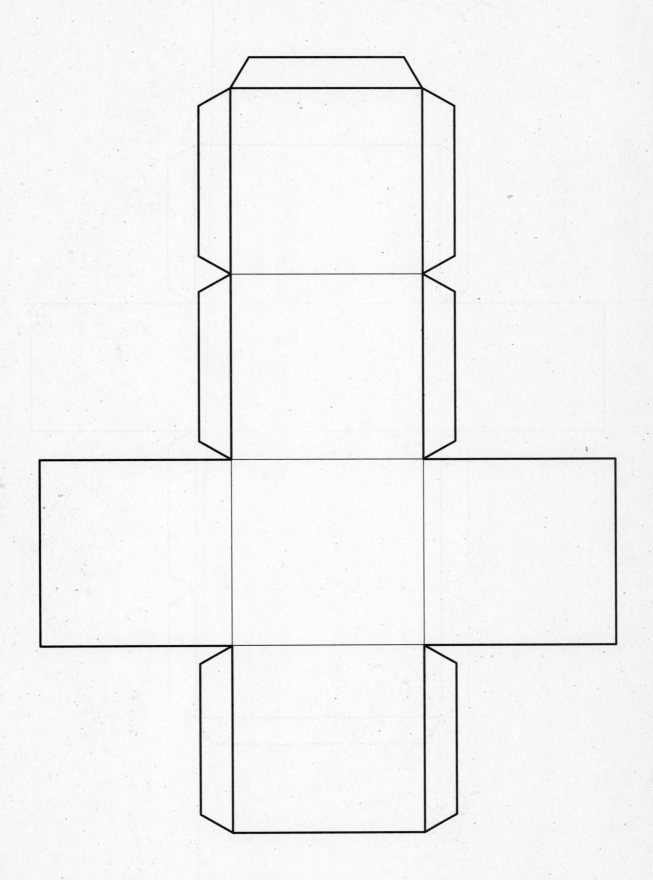

Cube Pattern

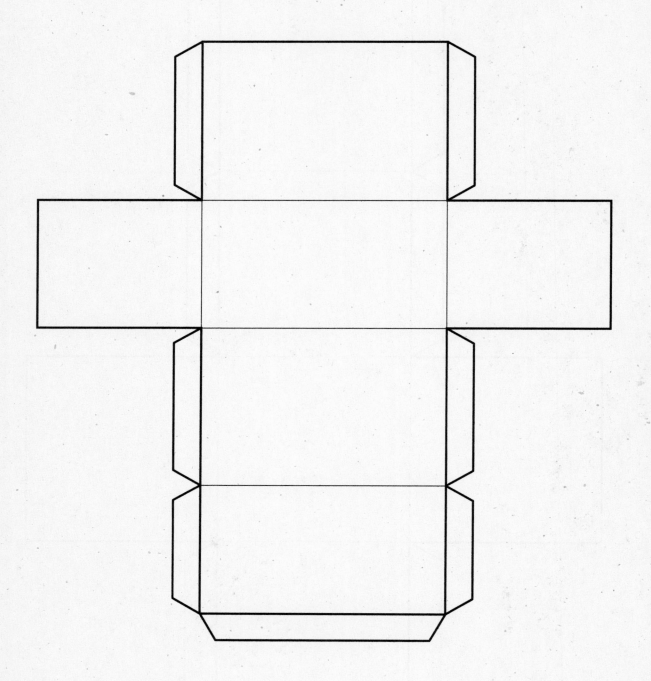

Rectangular Prism Pattern

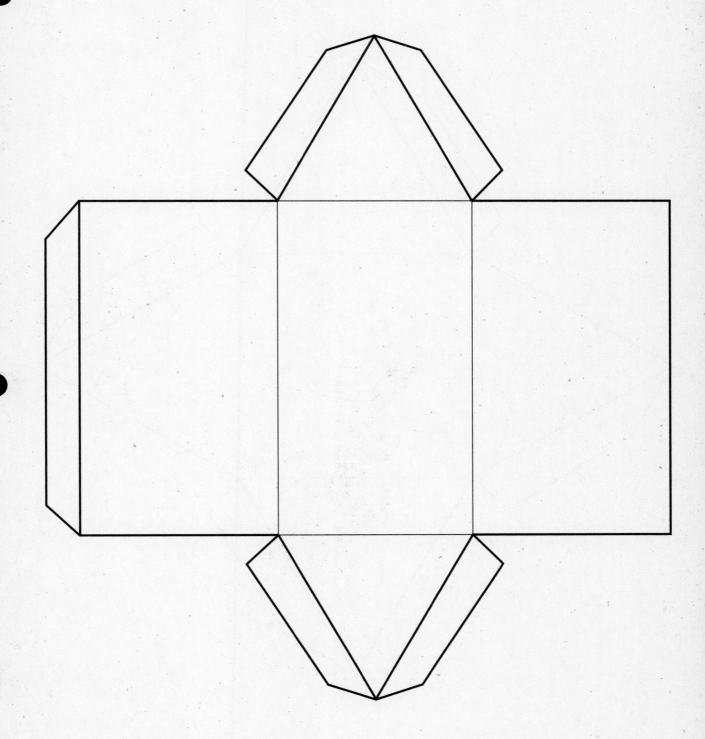

Triangular Prism Pattern

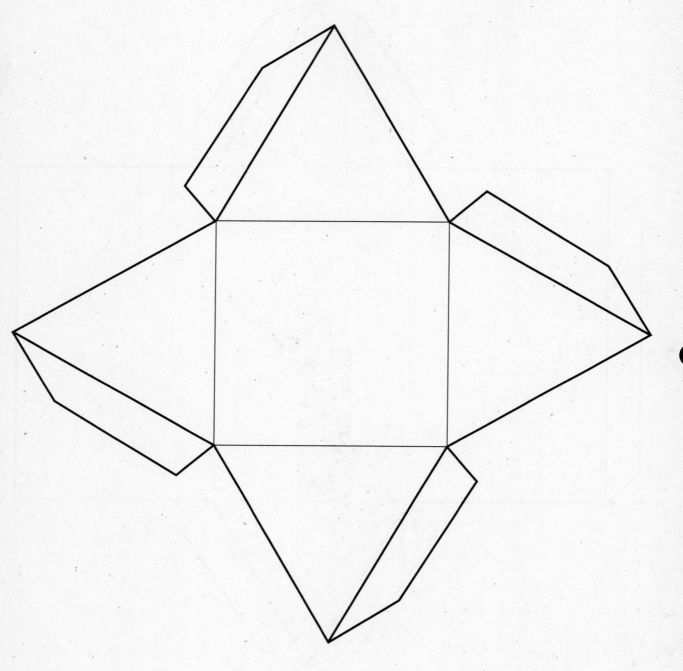

Square Pyramid Pattern

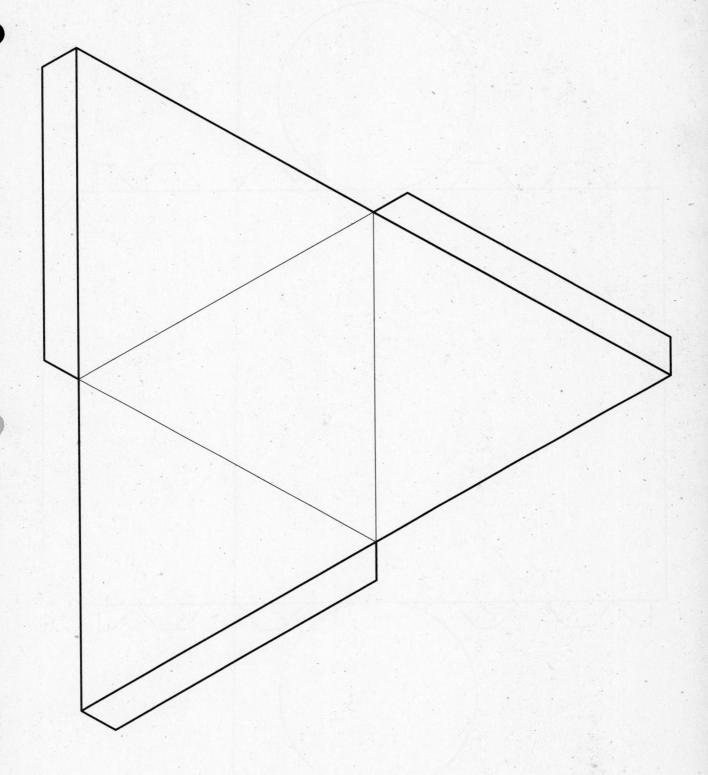

Triangular Pyramid Pattern

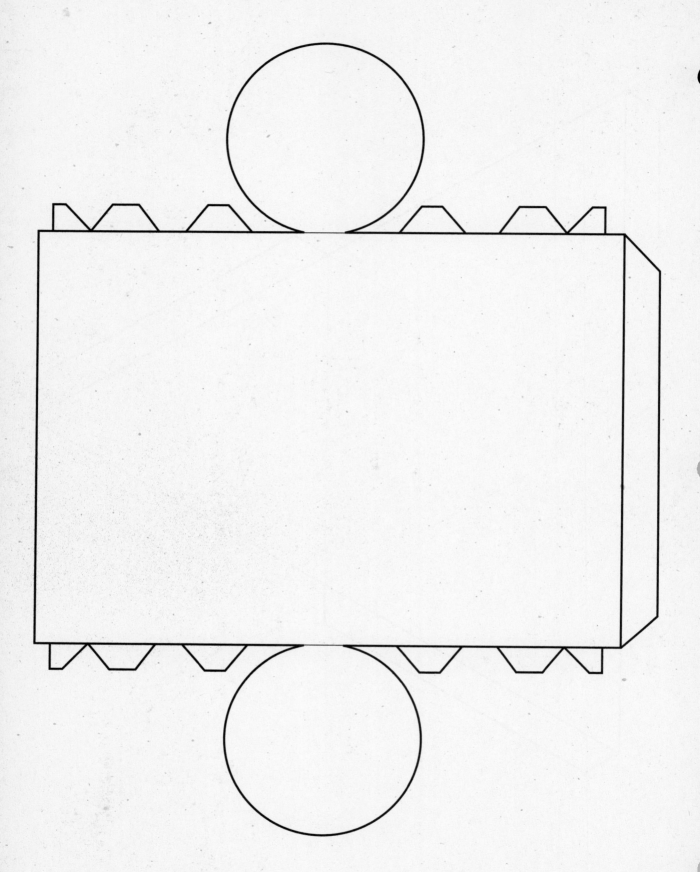

Cylinder Pattern

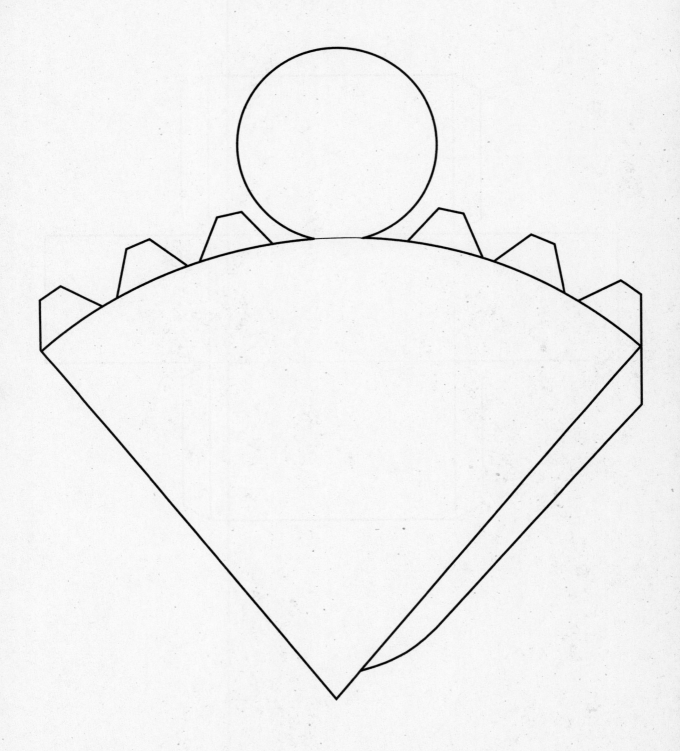

Cone Pattern

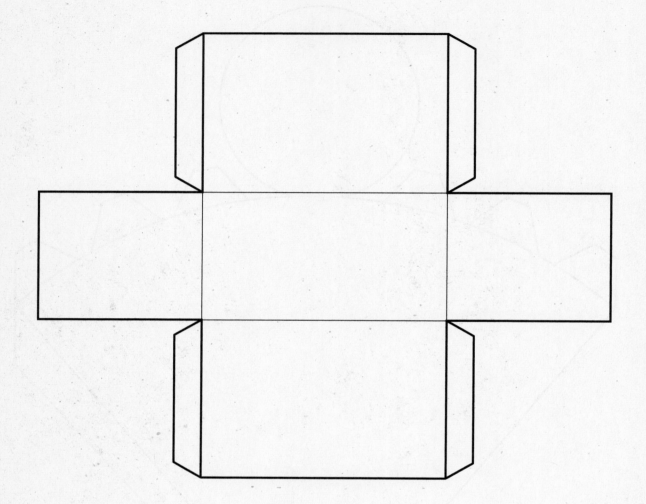

Open Rectangular Prism Pattern

Triangles

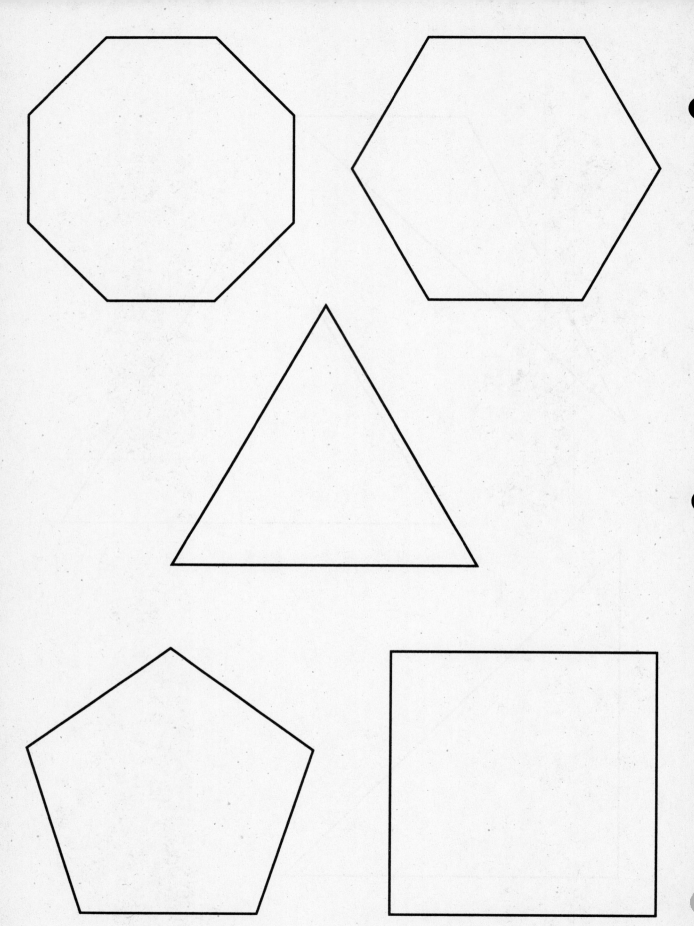

Plane Figures

© Harcourt

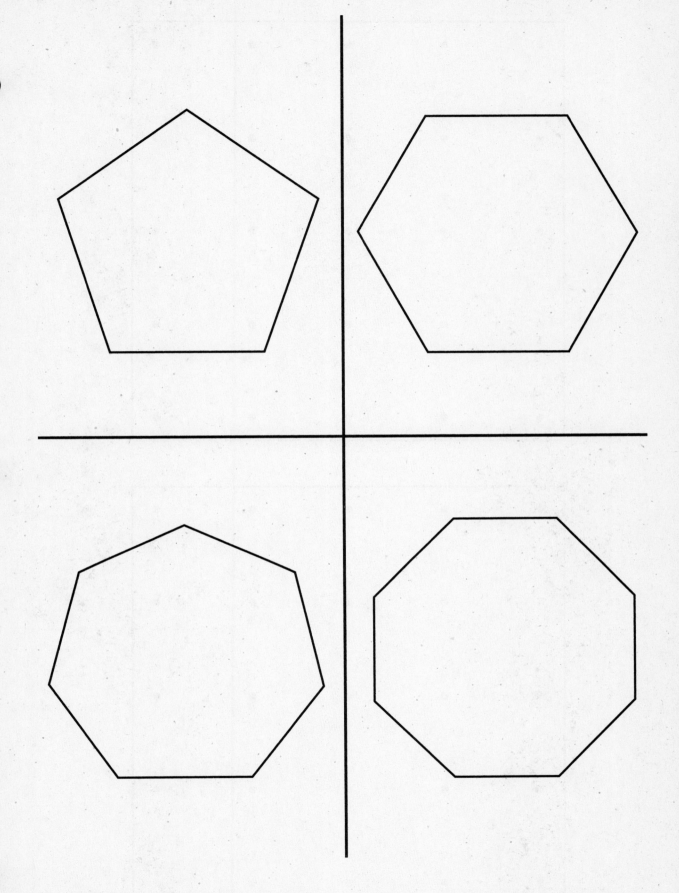

Polygons: Multi-sided

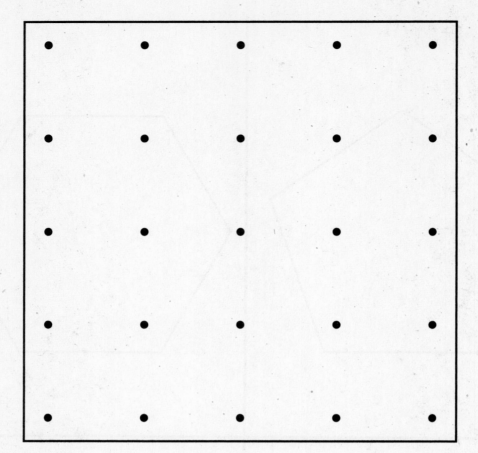

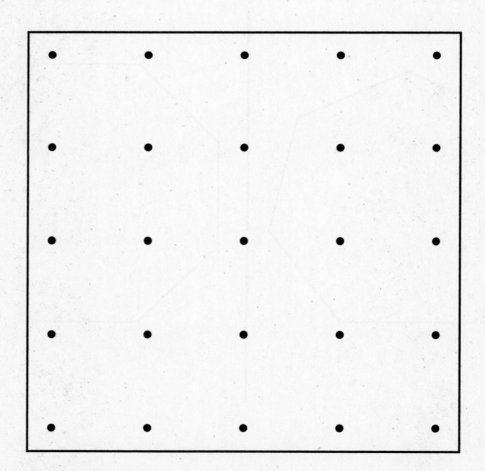

Geoboard Dot Paper

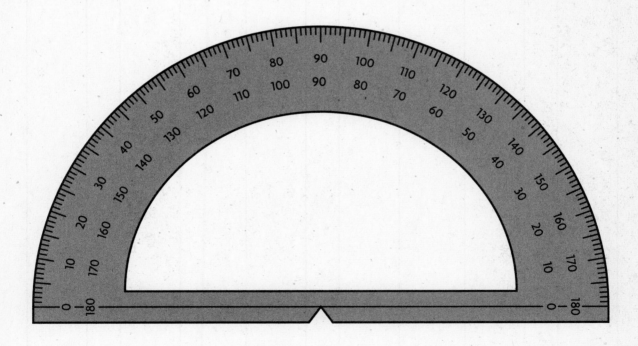

Protractors

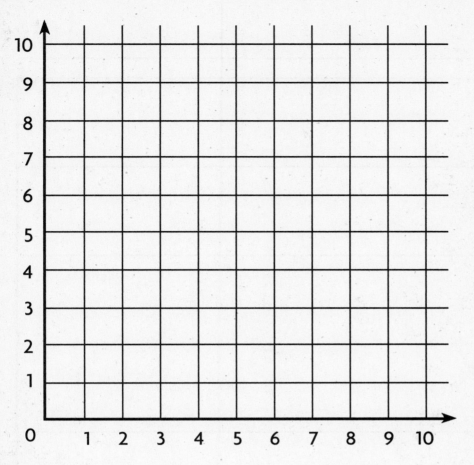

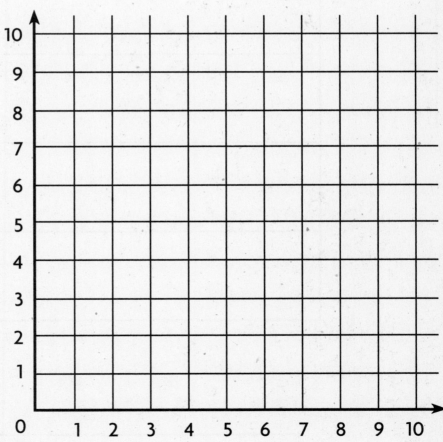

Grid of Quadrant I

Title _____

0

0

Title_____

0

Key

Title:

1-Centimeter Grid Paper

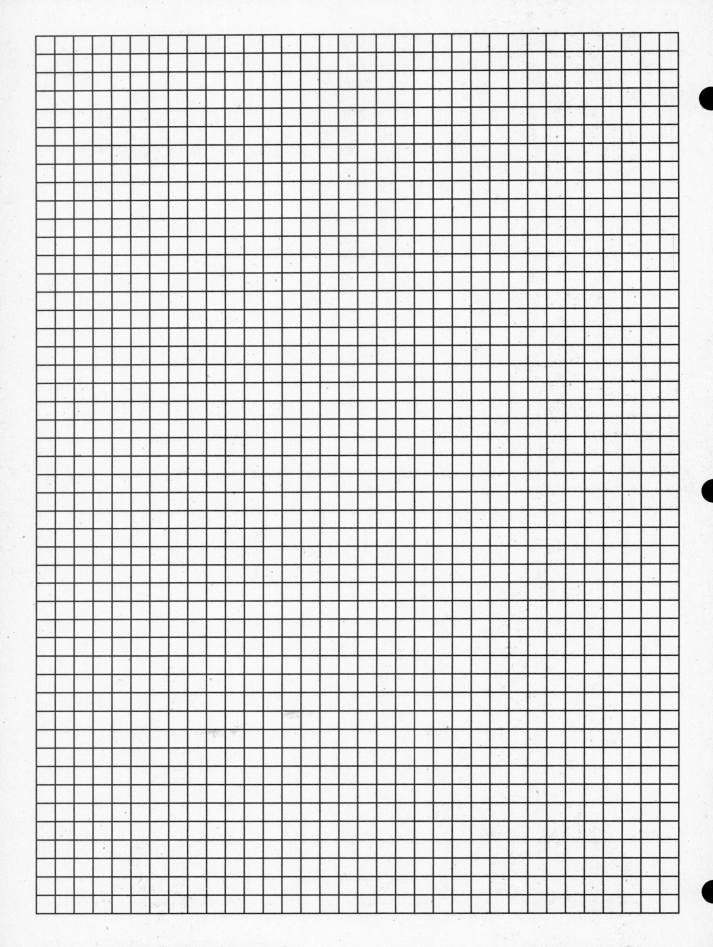

0.5-Centimeter Grid Paper

© Harcourt

	Tally	Frequency

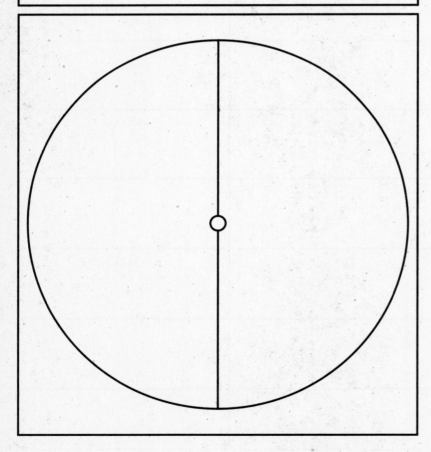

How to assemble spinner.
- Glue patterns to tagboard.
- Cut out and attach pointer with a fastener.

Alternative
- Students can use a paper clip and pencil instead.

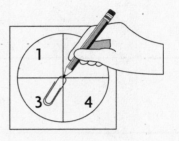

Spinners (blank and 2-section)

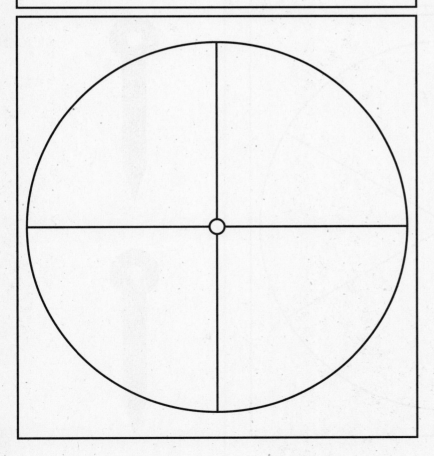

Spinner Tips

How to assemble spinner.
- Glue patterns to tagboard.
- Cut out and attach pointer with a fastener.

Alternative
- Students can use a paper clip and pencil instead.

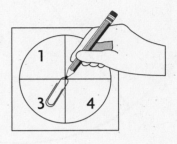

Spinners (3- and 4-section)

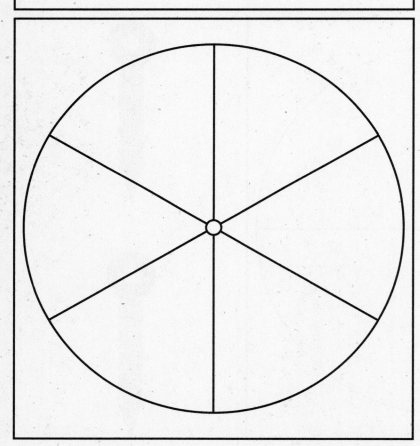

Spinner Tips

How to assemble spinner.
- Glue patterns to tagboard.
- Cut out and attach pointer with a fastener.

Alternative
- Students can use a paper clip and pencil instead.

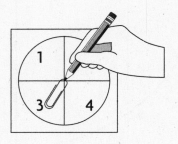

Spinners (5-and 6-section)

© Harcourt

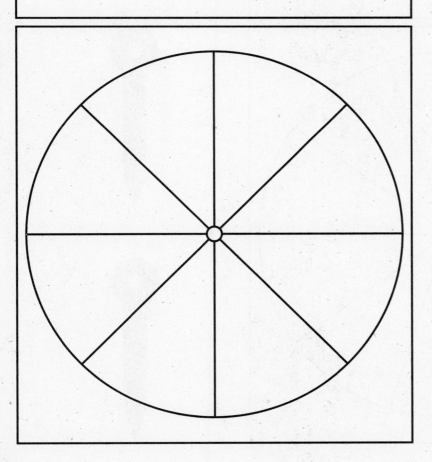

Spinner Tips

How to assemble spinner.
- Glue patterns to tagboard.
- Cut out and attach pointer with a fastener.

Alternative
- Students can use a paper clip and pencil instead.

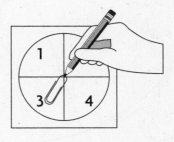

Spinners (7- and 8-section)

© Harcourt

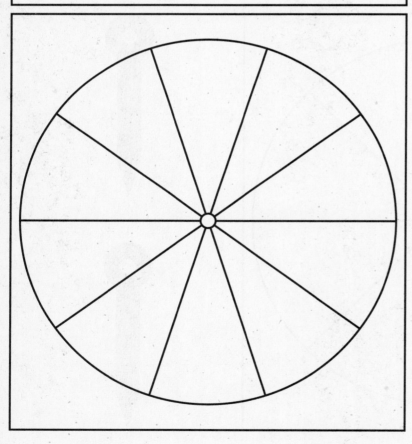

Spinner Tips

How to assemble spinner.
- Glue patterns to tagboard.
- Cut out and attach pointer with a fastener.

Alternative
- Students can use a paper clip and pencil instead.

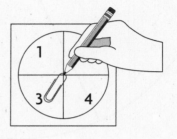

Spinners (9- and 10-section)

Number Cube Patterns

 **Put in order (least to greatest)**

 **Put in order (least to greatest)**

 **Put in order (greatest to least)**

Put in order (greatest to least)

COMPARE TWO

START *901* *910*	Lose 1 turn.	**89** **67**	200 600	**8,900** **9,800**
862 *866*	*299* *266*			**2,104** **2,401**
Toss Again.	**5,432** **4,321**			Go Back 2.
225 **265**	**10** **101**	*1,991* *1,091* **End**		**599** **549**
Go Ahead 2.				230 330
5,000 9,000	*123* *213*	*59* *53*	**162** **165**	Toss Again.

© Harcourt

Which kind of graph would best show the cost of a loaf of bread over the past 25 years? line graph	Which kind of graph would best show the field-trip choices of fourth graders? pictograph or bar graph	Which kind of graph would best compare two groups, such as a group of boys and a group of girls? double-bar graph
Which kind of graph would best show how many students were absent each month during the school year? line graph	Which kind of graph would best show the median age of teachers in your school? stem-and-leaf plot	Which kind of graph would best show the number of pages each of several students could read in an hour? pictograph or bar graph
Which kind of graph would best show the means of transportation each student uses for getting to school? pictograph or bar graph	Which kind of graph would best show the types of music enjoyed by students in a fourth-grade class? pictograph or bar graph	Which kind of graph would best compare the favorite sports of two classes? double-bar graph
Which kind of graph would best show the median number of sit-ups for students in your class? stem-and-leaf plot	Which kind of graph would best show the growth of a baby during the first year of life? line graph	Which kind of graph would best show the number of fourth graders who had visited famous places? pictograph or bar graph
Which kind of graph would best show the amount of rainfall over the past year? line graph	Which kind of graph would best show the median grade students in your class received on the math quiz? stem-and-leaf plot	Which kind of graph would best show the favorite authors of students in a fourth-grade class? pictograph or bar graph

Graph Score Sheet

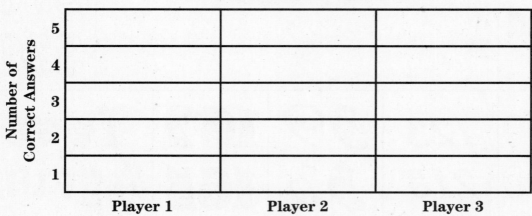

Graph Choice

✕	1	2	3	4	5	6	7	8	9
1	1	2	3	4	5	6	7	8	9
2	2	4	6	8	10	12	14	16	18
3	3	6	9	12	15	18	21	24	27
4	4	8	12	16	20	24	28	32	36
5	5	10	15	20	25	30	35	40	45
6	6	12	18	24	30	36	42	48	54
7	7	14	21	28	35	42	49	56	63
8	8	16	24	32	40	48	56	64	72
9	9	18	27	36	45	54	63	72	81

2	3
4	5
10	20
30	40
50	60

Shopping With Zeros

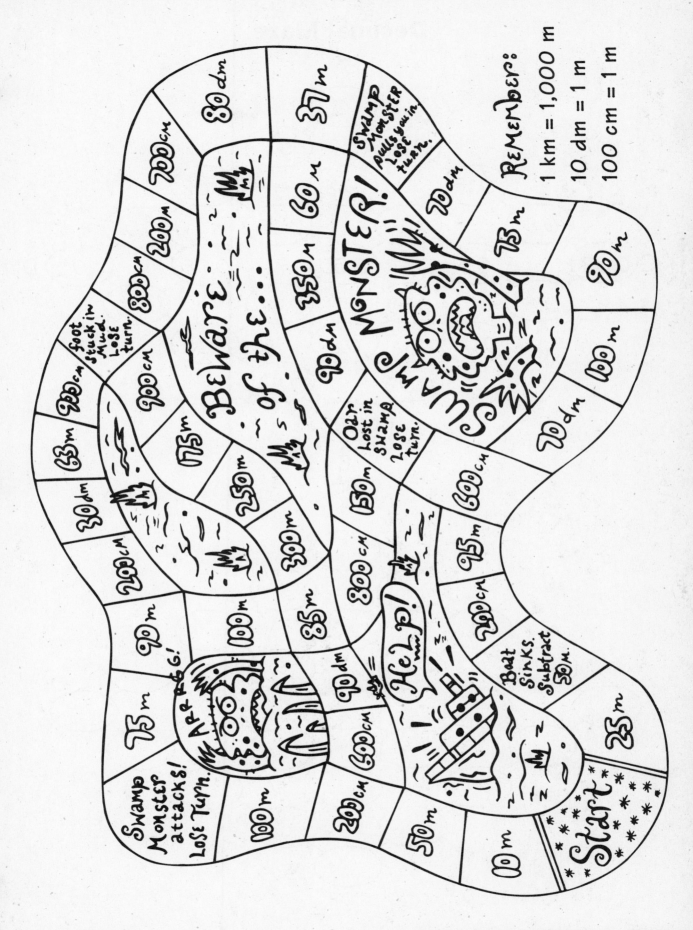

Beware of the Swamp Monster

Decimal Maze

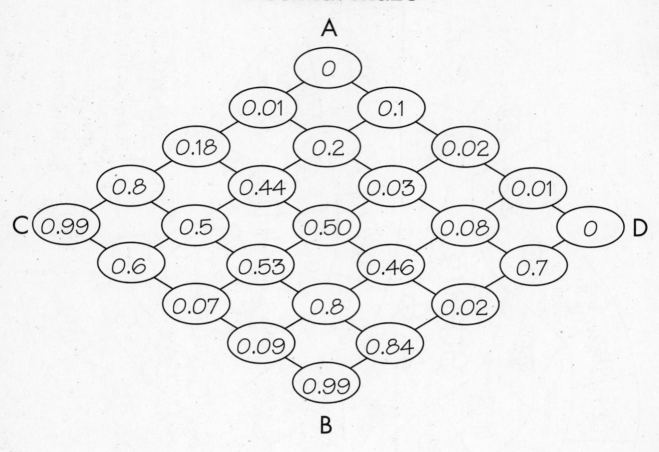

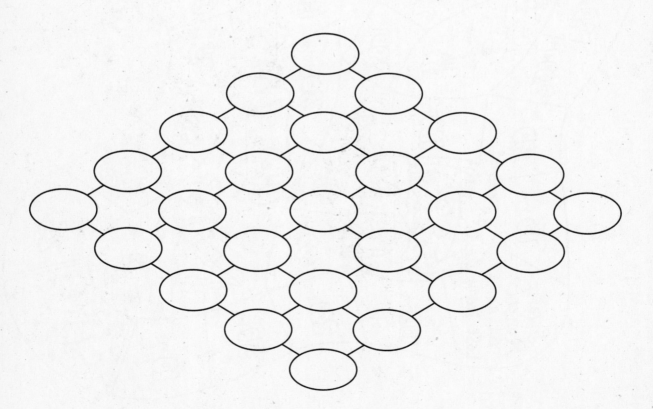

Decimal Maze

8	49	54
26	25	9
30	12	24

Perimeter	Area

Perimeter	Area
3 (square)	5 (square)
2 (square)	7 (square)
8 × 5 (rectangle)	9 × 6 (rectangle)
6 × 4 (rectangle)	7 × 5 (rectangle)

© Harcourt

BINGO

		FREE		

Bingo Grid

Math Award

To _____

For _____

_____

_____

By _____

EXCELLENCE

On this day of _____

Award Certificate

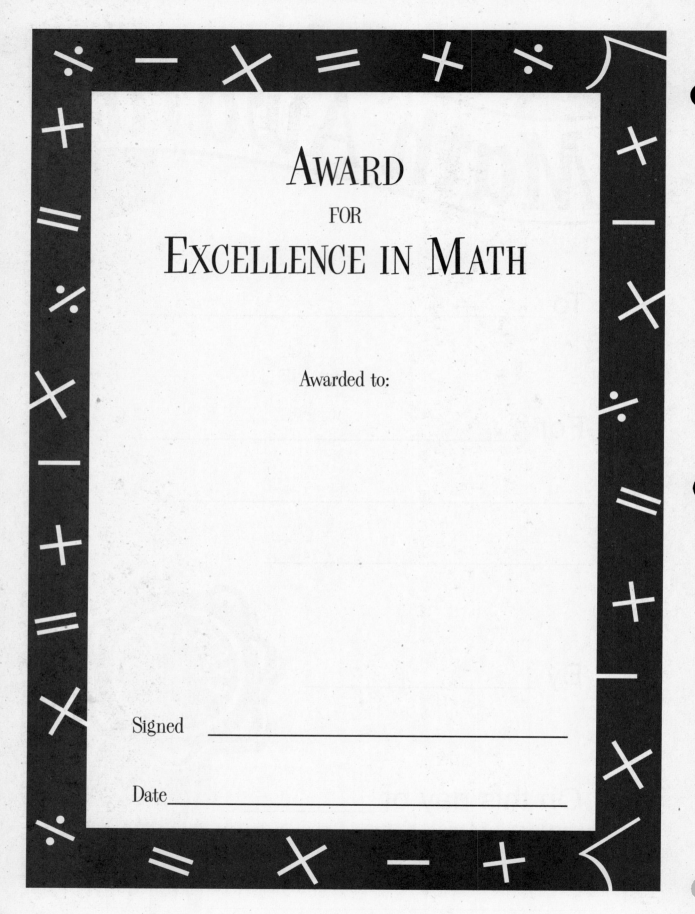

AWARD

FOR

EXCELLENCE IN MATH

Awarded to:

Signed _____

Date _____

© Harcourt

Award Certificate

Daily Facts Practice

A	0 +2	1 +3	10 +2	4 +2	5 +0	6 +10
B	4 −0	8 −2	6 −6	2 −1	9 −1	13 −3
C	2 +10	1 +0	9 +1	8 −8	19 −9	11 −2
D	1 ×5	9 ×0	7 ×1	3 ×3	0 ×5	2 ×4
E	6)0̅	2)2̅	1)7̅	1)0̅	10)30̅	2)10̅
F	1 ×8	10 ×4	3 ×2	7)7̅	9)0̅	6)12̅
G	2 +3	4 +5	7 +3	2 +6	10 +8	8 +5

Daily Facts Practice

A	$\begin{array}{r} 1 \\ \times 6 \\ \hline \end{array}$	$\begin{array}{r} 5 \\ \times 2 \\ \hline \end{array}$	$\begin{array}{r} 4 \\ \times 5 \\ \hline \end{array}$	$\begin{array}{r} 6 \\ \times 3 \\ \hline \end{array}$	$\begin{array}{r} 2 \\ \times 8 \\ \hline \end{array}$	$\begin{array}{r} 6 \\ \times 6 \\ \hline \end{array}$
B	$10\overline{)50}$	$3\overline{)9}$	$4\overline{)28}$	$\begin{array}{r} 0 \\ \times 9 \\ \hline \end{array}$	$\begin{array}{r} 8 \\ \times 4 \\ \hline \end{array}$	$\begin{array}{r} 10 \\ \times 6 \\ \hline \end{array}$
C	$\begin{array}{r} 6 \\ -4 \\ \hline \end{array}$	$\begin{array}{r} 11 \\ -6 \\ \hline \end{array}$	$\begin{array}{r} 8 \\ -7 \\ \hline \end{array}$	$\begin{array}{r} 9 \\ +7 \\ \hline \end{array}$	$\begin{array}{r} 6 \\ +3 \\ \hline \end{array}$	$\begin{array}{r} 4 \\ +8 \\ \hline \end{array}$
D	$\begin{array}{r} 9 \\ +2 \\ \hline \end{array}$	$\begin{array}{r} 2 \\ +1 \\ \hline \end{array}$	$\begin{array}{r} 3 \\ +4 \\ \hline \end{array}$	$\begin{array}{r} 7 \\ +6 \\ \hline \end{array}$	$\begin{array}{r} 7 \\ +8 \\ \hline \end{array}$	$\begin{array}{r} 5 \\ +10 \\ \hline \end{array}$
E	$\begin{array}{r} 5 \\ +4 \\ \hline \end{array}$	$\begin{array}{r} 9 \\ -6 \\ \hline \end{array}$	$\begin{array}{r} 0 \\ +7 \\ \hline \end{array}$	$\begin{array}{r} 13 \\ -5 \\ \hline \end{array}$	$\begin{array}{r} 5 \\ +7 \\ \hline \end{array}$	$\begin{array}{r} 11 \\ -7 \\ \hline \end{array}$
F	$\begin{array}{r} 4 \\ -2 \\ \hline \end{array}$	$\begin{array}{r} 8 \\ -3 \\ \hline \end{array}$	$\begin{array}{r} 6 \\ -1 \\ \hline \end{array}$	$\begin{array}{r} 9 \\ -4 \\ \hline \end{array}$	$\begin{array}{r} 12 \\ -8 \\ \hline \end{array}$	$\begin{array}{r} 19 \\ -10 \\ \hline \end{array}$
G	$\begin{array}{r} 17 \\ -7 \\ \hline \end{array}$	$\begin{array}{r} 6 \\ +9 \\ \hline \end{array}$	$\begin{array}{r} 8 \\ -5 \\ \hline \end{array}$	$\begin{array}{r} 10 \\ +4 \\ \hline \end{array}$	$\begin{array}{r} 13 \\ -6 \\ \hline \end{array}$	$\begin{array}{r} 7 \\ +4 \\ \hline \end{array}$

Daily Facts Practice

A	$\begin{array}{r}2\\+2\\\hline\end{array}$	$\begin{array}{r}6\\+6\\\hline\end{array}$	$\begin{array}{r}5\\+2\\\hline\end{array}$	$\begin{array}{r}10\\+0\\\hline\end{array}$	$\begin{array}{r}5\\+9\\\hline\end{array}$	$\begin{array}{r}9\\+9\\\hline\end{array}$
B	$\begin{array}{r}0\\\times10\\\hline\end{array}$	$\begin{array}{r}2\\\times7\\\hline\end{array}$	$\begin{array}{r}5\\\times9\\\hline\end{array}$	$\begin{array}{r}6\\\times4\\\hline\end{array}$	$\begin{array}{r}6\\\times8\\\hline\end{array}$	$\begin{array}{r}3\\\times9\\\hline\end{array}$
C	$\begin{array}{r}6\\\times5\\\hline\end{array}$	$\begin{array}{r}2\\\times3\\\hline\end{array}$	$\begin{array}{r}7\\\times0\\\hline\end{array}$	$\begin{array}{r}5\\\times5\\\hline\end{array}$	$\begin{array}{r}3\\\times8\\\hline\end{array}$	$\begin{array}{r}8\\\times9\\\hline\end{array}$
D	$10\overline{)90}$	$6\overline{)48}$	$5\overline{)20}$	$3\overline{)18}$	$8\overline{)64}$	$7\overline{)28}$
E	$2\overline{)6}$	$3\overline{)21}$	$2\overline{)20}$	$6\overline{)36}$	$7\overline{)42}$	$9\overline{)27}$
F	$8\overline{)40}$	$3\overline{)0}$	$6\overline{)60}$	$7\overline{)14}$	$9\overline{)54}$	$8\overline{)32}$
G	$\begin{array}{r}2\\+7\\\hline\end{array}$	$\begin{array}{r}3\\-2\\\hline\end{array}$	$\begin{array}{r}8\\-4\\\hline\end{array}$	$\begin{array}{r}12\\-2\\\hline\end{array}$	$\begin{array}{r}1\\+8\\\hline\end{array}$	$\begin{array}{r}8\\+10\\\hline\end{array}$

Daily Facts Practice

A	$\begin{array}{r} 12 \\ -5 \\ \hline \end{array}$	$\begin{array}{r} 6 \\ +8 \\ \hline \end{array}$	$\begin{array}{r} 10 \\ -7 \\ \hline \end{array}$	$\begin{array}{r} 2 \\ +5 \\ \hline \end{array}$	$\begin{array}{r} 1 \\ +6 \\ \hline \end{array}$	$\begin{array}{r} 14 \\ -7 \\ \hline \end{array}$
B	$\begin{array}{r} 4 \\ \times 6 \\ \hline \end{array}$	$4\overline{)36}$	$\begin{array}{r} 5 \\ \times 7 \\ \hline \end{array}$	$5\overline{)30}$	$\begin{array}{r} 9 \\ \times 7 \\ \hline \end{array}$	$1\overline{)10}$
C	$\begin{array}{r} 5 \\ +1 \\ \hline \end{array}$	$\begin{array}{r} 3 \\ +3 \\ \hline \end{array}$	$\begin{array}{r} 5 \\ +6 \\ \hline \end{array}$	$\begin{array}{r} 7 \\ +7 \\ \hline \end{array}$	$\begin{array}{r} 2 \\ +9 \\ \hline \end{array}$	$\begin{array}{r} 8 \\ +4 \\ \hline \end{array}$
D	$\begin{array}{r} 3 \\ +9 \\ \hline \end{array}$	$\begin{array}{r} 10 \\ +10 \\ \hline \end{array}$	$\begin{array}{r} 0 \\ +6 \\ \hline \end{array}$	$\begin{array}{r} 3 \\ +8 \\ \hline \end{array}$	$\begin{array}{r} 6 \\ +5 \\ \hline \end{array}$	$\begin{array}{r} 4 \\ +7 \\ \hline \end{array}$
E	$\begin{array}{r} 12 \\ -6 \\ \hline \end{array}$	$\begin{array}{r} 10 \\ -0 \\ \hline \end{array}$	$\begin{array}{r} 16 \\ -7 \\ \hline \end{array}$	$\begin{array}{r} 11 \\ -3 \\ \hline \end{array}$	$\begin{array}{r} 10 \\ -8 \\ \hline \end{array}$	$\begin{array}{r} 13 \\ -4 \\ \hline \end{array}$
F	$\begin{array}{r} 9 \\ +3 \\ \hline \end{array}$	$\begin{array}{r} 10 \\ -10 \\ \hline \end{array}$	$\begin{array}{r} 3 \\ +10 \\ \hline \end{array}$	$\begin{array}{r} 14 \\ -9 \\ \hline \end{array}$	$\begin{array}{r} 8 \\ +8 \\ \hline \end{array}$	$\begin{array}{r} 12 \\ -7 \\ \hline \end{array}$
G	$\begin{array}{r} 16 \\ -10 \\ \hline \end{array}$	$\begin{array}{r} 7 \\ -6 \\ \hline \end{array}$	$\begin{array}{r} 5 \\ -3 \\ \hline \end{array}$	$\begin{array}{r} 11 \\ -6 \\ \hline \end{array}$	$\begin{array}{r} 15 \\ -8 \\ \hline \end{array}$	$\begin{array}{r} 12 \\ -9 \\ \hline \end{array}$

Daily Facts Practice

A	10×10	2×6	8×5	9×2	7×6	9×3
B	$7 - 4$	$16 - 8$	$11 - 1$	$15 - 9$	$12 - 10$	$18 - 9$
C	$3 \overline{)30}$	8×7	$7 \overline{)63}$	7×10	$9 \overline{)81}$	4×4
D	$9 + 4$	$5 + 5$	$1 + 7$	$3 + 6$	$6 + 2$	$8 + 7$
E	$10 + 7$	$4 + 4$	$8 + 3$	$1 + 2$	$8 + 6$	$9 + 8$
F	$3 + 2$	$15 - 7$	$10 - 9$	$9 + 5$	$4 + 6$	$9 - 3$
G	$11 - 10$	$13 - 8$	$7 - 5$	$10 - 3$	$5 - 2$	$11 - 8$

Daily Facts Practice

A	5 +3	7 +1	13 −7	0 +5	6 −5	14 −8
B	20 −10	17 −9	10 +5	6 +7	8 −6	7 −3
C	4 −4	10 −6	14 −5	9 −8	13 −9	10 −4
D	7 ×8	4 ×9	4 ×7	$8\overline{)16}$	$5\overline{)45}$	$4\overline{)24}$
E	$4\overline{)8}$	$3\overline{)24}$	7 ×2	5 ×10	$6\overline{)24}$	$9\overline{)63}$
F	3 ×1	7 ×5	$5\overline{)50}$	$4\overline{)20}$	6 ×9	9 ×4
G	10 ×1	8 ×3	6 ×7	4 ×8	2 ×9	7 ×9

Daily Facts Practice

A	2 ×2	8 ×6	3 ×5	7 ×4	7 ×3	9 ×6

B	2)‾18	4)‾40	10 ×5	7 ×7	6)‾30	9)‾72

C	7 +9	5 +8	4 +3	11 −4	14 −6	12 −3

D	2 +4	4 +9	10 +3	2 +9	7 +5	8 +2

E	4 ×3	5 ×0	3 ×6	8 ×8	5 ×4	9 ×5

F	4 ×2	5 ×8	3 ×7	10 ×8	8 ×2	9 ×8

G	15 −10	7 −2	11 −9	10 −5	12 −4	9 −2

Daily Facts Practice

A	$\begin{array}{r} 16 \\ -6 \\ \hline \end{array}$	$\begin{array}{r} 6 \\ -3 \\ \hline \end{array}$	$\begin{array}{r} 9 \\ -5 \\ \hline \end{array}$	$\begin{array}{r} 17 \\ -10 \\ \hline \end{array}$	$\begin{array}{r} 16 \\ -9 \\ \hline \end{array}$	$\begin{array}{r} 10 \\ -2 \\ \hline \end{array}$
B	$\begin{array}{r} 5 \\ \times 3 \\ \hline \end{array}$	$\begin{array}{r} 9 \\ \times 9 \\ \hline \end{array}$	$\begin{array}{r} 6 \\ \times 2 \\ \hline \end{array}$	$2\overline{)16}$	$5\overline{)35}$	$7\overline{)49}$
C	$5\overline{)25}$	$8\overline{)72}$	$9\overline{)18}$	$\begin{array}{r} 5 \\ \times 3 \\ \hline \end{array}$	$\begin{array}{r} 9 \\ \times 9 \\ \hline \end{array}$	$\begin{array}{r} 6 \\ \times 2 \\ \hline \end{array}$
D	$2\overline{)8}$	$\begin{array}{r} 2 \\ \times 11 \\ \hline \end{array}$	$3\overline{)27}$	$\begin{array}{r} 5 \\ \times 6 \\ \hline \end{array}$	$5\overline{)55}$	$\begin{array}{r} 3 \\ \times 4 \\ \hline \end{array}$
E	$\begin{array}{r} 2 \\ \times 5 \\ \hline \end{array}$	$\begin{array}{r} 11 \\ \times 0 \\ \hline \end{array}$	$\begin{array}{r} 12 \\ \times 2 \\ \hline \end{array}$	$\begin{array}{r} 10 \\ \times 3 \\ \hline \end{array}$	$\begin{array}{r} 7 \\ \times 6 \\ \hline \end{array}$	$\begin{array}{r} 6 \\ \times 11 \\ \hline \end{array}$
F	$\begin{array}{r} 2 \\ \times 6 \\ \hline \end{array}$	$\begin{array}{r} 9 \\ \times 1 \\ \hline \end{array}$	$\begin{array}{r} 12 \\ \times 4 \\ \hline \end{array}$	$\begin{array}{r} 3 \\ \times 7 \\ \hline \end{array}$	$\begin{array}{r} 6 \\ \times 9 \\ \hline \end{array}$	$\begin{array}{r} 3 \\ \times 8 \\ \hline \end{array}$
G	$\begin{array}{r} 8 \\ \times 10 \\ \hline \end{array}$	$\begin{array}{r} 11 \\ \times 2 \\ \hline \end{array}$	$\begin{array}{r} 4 \\ \times 4 \\ \hline \end{array}$	$\begin{array}{r} 8 \\ \times 5 \\ \hline \end{array}$	$\begin{array}{r} 6 \\ \times 4 \\ \hline \end{array}$	$\begin{array}{r} 5 \\ \times 12 \\ \hline \end{array}$

Daily Facts Practice

A	$\begin{array}{r} 0 \\ \times 7 \\ \hline \end{array}$	$3\overline{)6}$	$\begin{array}{r} 9 \\ \times 8 \\ \hline \end{array}$	$9\overline{)45}$	$\begin{array}{r} 7 \\ \times 3 \\ \hline \end{array}$	$11\overline{)55}$
B	$\begin{array}{r} 4 \\ \times 2 \\ \hline \end{array}$	$\begin{array}{r} 12 \\ \times 3 \\ \hline \end{array}$	$\begin{array}{r} 4 \\ \times 5 \\ \hline \end{array}$	$\begin{array}{r} 8 \\ \times 7 \\ \hline \end{array}$	$\begin{array}{r} 2 \\ \times 9 \\ \hline \end{array}$	$\begin{array}{r} 8 \\ \times 8 \\ \hline \end{array}$
C	$\begin{array}{r} 7 \\ +2 \\ \hline \end{array}$	$\begin{array}{r} 4 \\ -3 \\ \hline \end{array}$	$\begin{array}{r} 6 \\ +4 \\ \hline \end{array}$	$\begin{array}{r} 14 \\ -10 \\ \hline \end{array}$	$\begin{array}{r} 8 \\ +9 \\ \hline \end{array}$	$\begin{array}{r} 15 \\ -6 \\ \hline \end{array}$
D	$\begin{array}{r} 4 \\ \times 12 \\ \hline \end{array}$	$\begin{array}{r} 8 \\ \times 11 \\ \hline \end{array}$	$\begin{array}{r} 4 \\ \times 1 \\ \hline \end{array}$	$\begin{array}{r} 3 \\ \times 3 \\ \hline \end{array}$	$\begin{array}{r} 1 \\ \times 10 \\ \hline \end{array}$	$\begin{array}{r} 6 \\ \times 12 \\ \hline \end{array}$
E	$3\overline{)36}$	$11\overline{)77}$	$\begin{array}{r} 11 \\ \times 9 \\ \hline \end{array}$	$7\overline{)84}$	$11\overline{)110}$	$\begin{array}{r} 11 \\ \times 10 \\ \hline \end{array}$
F	$4\overline{)16}$	$7\overline{)21}$	$\begin{array}{r} 12 \\ \times 8 \\ \hline \end{array}$	$6\overline{)54}$	$9\overline{)90}$	$\begin{array}{r} 4 \\ \times 4 \\ \hline \end{array}$
G	$\begin{array}{r} 2 \\ +8 \\ \hline \end{array}$	$\begin{array}{r} 9 \\ +6 \\ \hline \end{array}$	$\begin{array}{r} 3 \\ +7 \\ \hline \end{array}$	$\begin{array}{r} 9 \\ -7 \\ \hline \end{array}$	$\begin{array}{r} 6 \\ -2 \\ \hline \end{array}$	$\begin{array}{r} 17 \\ -8 \\ \hline \end{array}$

Daily Facts Practice

A	$11 \\ \times 3$	$7 \\ \times 7$	$2 \\ \times 10$	$2 \\ \times 12$	$6 \\ \times 5$	$12 \\ \times 10$
B	$1 \\ \times 4$	$7 \\ \times 11$	$8 \\ \times 9$	$10 \\ \times 11$	$12 \\ \times 6$	$11 \\ \times 12$
C	$9 \\ \times 7$	$4 \\ \times 11$	$3 \\ \times 4$	$4 \\ \times 8$	$12 \\ \times 5$	$9 \\ \times 12$
D	$8\overline{)88}$	$8 \\ \times 2$	$3 \\ \times 12$	$6 \\ \times 6$	$9 \\ \times 3$	$2\overline{)12}$
E	$7 \\ \times 12$	$8\overline{)56}$	$0 \\ \times 8$	$4\overline{)32}$	$2 \\ \times 5$	$5\overline{)60}$
F	$2\overline{)14}$	$11\overline{)44}$	$12\overline{)48}$	$6\overline{)42}$	$7\overline{)77}$	$8\overline{)48}$
G	$9\overline{)99}$	$5\overline{)0}$	$4\overline{)48}$	$7\overline{)56}$	$2\overline{)24}$	$8\overline{)80}$

Daily Facts Practice

A	$8\overline{)24}$	$2\overline{)4}$	$6\overline{)72}$	$11\overline{)121}$	$9\overline{)36}$	$10\overline{)70}$
B	$5\overline{)40}$	$\begin{array}{r} 5 \\ \times 11 \\ \hline \end{array}$	$6\overline{)66}$	$\begin{array}{r} 12 \\ \times 9 \\ \hline \end{array}$	$12\overline{)84}$	$\begin{array}{r} 9 \\ \times 10 \\ \hline \end{array}$
C	$3\overline{)12}$	$6\overline{)18}$	$7\overline{)35}$	$12\overline{)96}$	$11\overline{)22}$	$10\overline{)120}$
D	$\begin{array}{r} 18 \\ -10 \\ \hline \end{array}$	$\begin{array}{r} 5 \\ -4 \\ \hline \end{array}$	$\begin{array}{r} 11 \\ -6 \\ \hline \end{array}$	$\begin{array}{r} 15 \\ -7 \\ \hline \end{array}$	$\begin{array}{r} 10 \\ -4 \\ \hline \end{array}$	$\begin{array}{r} 7 \\ -1 \\ \hline \end{array}$
E	$\begin{array}{r} 9 \\ -7 \\ \hline \end{array}$	$\begin{array}{r} 14 \\ -9 \\ \hline \end{array}$	$\begin{array}{r} 7 \\ -0 \\ \hline \end{array}$	$\begin{array}{r} 9 \\ -3 \\ \hline \end{array}$	$\begin{array}{r} 15 \\ -8 \\ \hline \end{array}$	$\begin{array}{r} 14 \\ -5 \\ \hline \end{array}$
F	$3\overline{)15}$	$4\overline{)44}$	$12\overline{)72}$	$8\overline{)96}$	$7\overline{)70}$	$5\overline{)15}$
G	$5\overline{)10}$	$11\overline{)99}$	$10\overline{)100}$	$4\overline{)12}$	$7\overline{)63}$	$9\overline{)27}$

Daily Facts Practice

A	$6\overline{)30}$	$12\overline{)144}$	$3\overline{)33}$	$10\overline{)110}$	$12\overline{)36}$	$9\overline{)54}$

B	$\begin{array}{r}8\\ \times12\\ \hline\end{array}$	$\begin{array}{r}11\\ \times8\\ \hline\end{array}$	$\begin{array}{r}4\\ \times9\\ \hline\end{array}$	$\begin{array}{r}8\\ \times3\\ \hline\end{array}$	$\begin{array}{r}11\\ \times11\\ \hline\end{array}$	$\begin{array}{r}4\\ \times10\\ \hline\end{array}$

C	$\begin{array}{r}13\\ -10\\ \hline\end{array}$	$\begin{array}{r}7\\ -4\\ \hline\end{array}$	$\begin{array}{r}11\\ -2\\ \hline\end{array}$	$\begin{array}{r}15\\ -5\\ \hline\end{array}$	$\begin{array}{r}11\\ -3\\ \hline\end{array}$	$\begin{array}{r}14\\ -6\\ \hline\end{array}$

D	$\begin{array}{r}9\\ \times11\\ \hline\end{array}$	$\begin{array}{r}12\\ \times7\\ \hline\end{array}$	$12\overline{)24}$	$\begin{array}{r}9\\ \times6\\ \hline\end{array}$	$\begin{array}{r}10\\ \times2\\ \hline\end{array}$	$9\overline{)108}$

E	$2\overline{)22}$	$9\overline{)9}$	$12\overline{)132}$	$11\overline{)0}$	$7\overline{)28}$	$5\overline{)45}$

F	$11\overline{)66}$	$9\overline{)72}$	$4\overline{)32}$	$3\overline{)21}$	$11\overline{)11}$	$8\overline{)64}$

G	$10\overline{)40}$	$8\overline{)48}$	$6\overline{)24}$	$5\overline{)35}$	$12\overline{)120}$	$3\overline{)27}$

Daily Facts Practice

A	$12\overline{)60}$	$11\overline{)88}$	$\begin{array}{r} 7 \\ \times 4 \\ \hline \end{array}$	$5\overline{)25}$	$4\overline{)36}$	$\begin{array}{r} 12 \\ \times 12 \\ \hline \end{array}$
B	$\begin{array}{r} 3 \\ \times 10 \\ \hline \end{array}$	$\begin{array}{r} 5 \\ \times 7 \\ \hline \end{array}$	$\begin{array}{r} 0 \\ \times 6 \\ \hline \end{array}$	$8\overline{)8}$	$7\overline{)56}$	$2\overline{)14}$
C	$10\overline{)80}$	$12\overline{)108}$	$3\overline{)15}$	$6\overline{)54}$	$10\overline{)60}$	$8\overline{)96}$
D	$\begin{array}{r} 6 \\ +9 \\ \hline \end{array}$	$\begin{array}{r} 8 \\ +8 \\ \hline \end{array}$	$\begin{array}{r} 7 \\ +2 \\ \hline \end{array}$	$\begin{array}{r} 10 \\ +9 \\ \hline \end{array}$	$\begin{array}{r} 3 \\ +5 \\ \hline \end{array}$	$\begin{array}{r} 6 \\ +7 \\ \hline \end{array}$
E	$\begin{array}{r} 10 \\ +6 \\ \hline \end{array}$	$\begin{array}{r} 5 \\ +6 \\ \hline \end{array}$	$\begin{array}{r} 8 \\ +4 \\ \hline \end{array}$	$\begin{array}{r} 9 \\ +7 \\ \hline \end{array}$	$\begin{array}{r} 4 \\ +5 \\ \hline \end{array}$	$\begin{array}{r} 9 \\ +5 \\ \hline \end{array}$
F	$\begin{array}{r} 18 \\ -8 \\ \hline \end{array}$	$\begin{array}{r} 13 \\ -9 \\ \hline \end{array}$	$\begin{array}{r} 15 \\ -6 \\ \hline \end{array}$	$\begin{array}{r} 6 \\ -4 \\ \hline \end{array}$	$\begin{array}{r} 10 \\ -2 \\ \hline \end{array}$	$\begin{array}{r} 13 \\ -8 \\ \hline \end{array}$
G	$\begin{array}{r} 17 \\ -10 \\ \hline \end{array}$	$\begin{array}{r} 11 \\ -6 \\ \hline \end{array}$	$\begin{array}{r} 8 \\ -2 \\ \hline \end{array}$	$\begin{array}{r} 12 \\ -9 \\ \hline \end{array}$	$\begin{array}{r} 16 \\ -8 \\ \hline \end{array}$	$\begin{array}{r} 14 \\ -7 \\ \hline \end{array}$

Daily Facts Practice

A	$\begin{array}{r}3\\+9\\\hline\end{array}$	$\begin{array}{r}8\\+6\\\hline\end{array}$	$\begin{array}{r}7\\+5\\\hline\end{array}$	$\begin{array}{r}9\\+2\\\hline\end{array}$	$\begin{array}{r}4\\+7\\\hline\end{array}$	$\begin{array}{r}9\\+9\\\hline\end{array}$
B	$\begin{array}{r}12\\\times11\\\hline\end{array}$	$\begin{array}{r}3\\\times6\\\hline\end{array}$	$\begin{array}{r}2\\\times4\\\hline\end{array}$	$\begin{array}{r}11\\\times6\\\hline\end{array}$	$\begin{array}{r}3\\\times9\\\hline\end{array}$	$\begin{array}{r}5\\\times8\\\hline\end{array}$
C	$11\overline{)132}$	$8\overline{)24}$	$\begin{array}{r}3\\\times11\\\hline\end{array}$	$\begin{array}{r}10\\\times7\\\hline\end{array}$	$4\overline{)20}$	$9\overline{)90}$
D	$12\overline{)12}$	$8\overline{)16}$	$6\overline{)48}$	$5\overline{)15}$	$3\overline{)24}$	$12\overline{)48}$
E	$11\overline{)66}$	$\begin{array}{r}2\\\times7\\\hline\end{array}$	$7\overline{)21}$	$\begin{array}{r}10\\\times12\\\hline\end{array}$	$4\overline{)28}$	$\begin{array}{r}7\\\times9\\\hline\end{array}$
F	$\begin{array}{r}3\\+8\\\hline\end{array}$	$\begin{array}{r}8\\+9\\\hline\end{array}$	$\begin{array}{r}7\\+10\\\hline\end{array}$	$\begin{array}{r}7\\+7\\\hline\end{array}$	$\begin{array}{r}5\\+9\\\hline\end{array}$	$\begin{array}{r}2\\+4\\\hline\end{array}$
G	$\begin{array}{r}12\\-5\\\hline\end{array}$	$\begin{array}{r}18\\-9\\\hline\end{array}$	$\begin{array}{r}10\\-3\\\hline\end{array}$	$\begin{array}{r}14\\-4\\\hline\end{array}$	$\begin{array}{r}15\\-9\\\hline\end{array}$	$\begin{array}{r}12\\-7\\\hline\end{array}$

Daily Facts Practice

A	7 +8	8 +5	9 +10	17 −8	10 −5	13 −7
B	16 −10	13 −5	8 −3	9 +8	7 +3	0 +10
C	10 +6	8 +7	4 +6	2 +8	4 +3	7 +9
D	16 −7	9 −5	12 −4	6 −5	13 −6	11 −7
E	11 −4	9 −6	16 −9	7 +4	3 +6	9 +7
F	7 ×8	7 ×12	5 ×6	9 ×4	12 ×3	2 ×8
G	11 ×7	9 ×9	6 ×7	7 ×5	6 ×3	4 ×12

Daily Facts Practice

A	$9\overline{)63}$	$12\overline{)96}$	$5\overline{)30}$	$2\overline{)16}$	$7\overline{)42}$	$8\overline{)88}$
B	$\begin{array}{r} 4 \\ \times 7 \\ \hline \end{array}$	$\begin{array}{r} 5 \\ \times 12 \\ \hline \end{array}$	$\begin{array}{r} 6 \\ \times 8 \\ \hline \end{array}$	$11\overline{)33}$	$9\overline{)36}$	$6\overline{)36}$
C	$\begin{array}{r} 6 \\ +8 \\ \hline \end{array}$	$\begin{array}{r} 14 \\ -10 \\ \hline \end{array}$	$\begin{array}{r} 10 \\ -7 \\ \hline \end{array}$	$\begin{array}{r} 13 \\ -4 \\ \hline \end{array}$	$\begin{array}{r} 9 \\ -4 \\ \hline \end{array}$	$\begin{array}{r} 10 \\ +1 \\ \hline \end{array}$
D	$\begin{array}{r} 2 \\ +5 \\ \hline \end{array}$	$\begin{array}{r} 6 \\ +6 \\ \hline \end{array}$	$\begin{array}{r} 9 \\ +4 \\ \hline \end{array}$	$\begin{array}{r} 5 \\ +7 \\ \hline \end{array}$	$\begin{array}{r} 6 \\ +4 \\ \hline \end{array}$	$\begin{array}{r} 9 \\ +3 \\ \hline \end{array}$
E	$\begin{array}{r} 4 \\ +10 \\ \hline \end{array}$	$\begin{array}{r} 11 \\ -9 \\ \hline \end{array}$	$\begin{array}{r} 8 \\ -7 \\ \hline \end{array}$	$\begin{array}{r} 12 \\ -6 \\ \hline \end{array}$	$\begin{array}{r} 7 \\ -3 \\ \hline \end{array}$	$\begin{array}{r} 5 \\ +8 \\ \hline \end{array}$
F	$\begin{array}{r} 9 \\ +6 \\ \hline \end{array}$	$\begin{array}{r} 8 \\ +3 \\ \hline \end{array}$	$\begin{array}{r} 4 \\ +8 \\ \hline \end{array}$	$\begin{array}{r} 5 \\ +5 \\ \hline \end{array}$	$\begin{array}{r} 7 \\ +6 \\ \hline \end{array}$	$\begin{array}{r} 2 \\ +3 \\ \hline \end{array}$
G	$\begin{array}{r} 17 \\ -9 \\ \hline \end{array}$	$\begin{array}{r} 11 \\ -8 \\ \hline \end{array}$	$\begin{array}{r} 9 \\ -2 \\ \hline \end{array}$	$\begin{array}{r} 10 \\ -9 \\ \hline \end{array}$	$\begin{array}{r} 7 \\ -2 \\ \hline \end{array}$	$\begin{array}{r} 14 \\ -8 \\ \hline \end{array}$

Daily Facts Practice

A	$\begin{array}{r} 3 \\ +7 \\ \hline \end{array}$	$\begin{array}{r} 8 \\ +2 \\ \hline \end{array}$	$\begin{array}{r} 12 \\ -8 \\ \hline \end{array}$	$\begin{array}{r} 1 \\ +9 \\ \hline \end{array}$	$\begin{array}{r} 10 \\ -6 \\ \hline \end{array}$	$\begin{array}{r} 7 \\ -5 \\ \hline \end{array}$
B	$\begin{array}{r} 4 \\ +9 \\ \hline \end{array}$	$\begin{array}{r} 8 \\ -5 \\ \hline \end{array}$	$\begin{array}{r} 10 \\ -8 \\ \hline \end{array}$	$\begin{array}{r} 6 \\ +5 \\ \hline \end{array}$	$\begin{array}{r} 4 \\ +2 \\ \hline \end{array}$	$\begin{array}{r} 12 \\ -3 \\ \hline \end{array}$
C	$\begin{array}{r} 12 \\ \times 4 \\ \hline \end{array}$	$\begin{array}{r} 5 \\ \times 9 \\ \hline \end{array}$	$\begin{array}{r} 8 \\ \times 4 \\ \hline \end{array}$	$\begin{array}{r} 4 \\ \times 3 \\ \hline \end{array}$	$\begin{array}{r} 11 \\ \times 5 \\ \hline \end{array}$	$\begin{array}{r} 8 \\ \times 6 \\ \hline \end{array}$
D	$\begin{array}{r} 6 \\ \times 2 \\ \hline \end{array}$	$\begin{array}{r} 12 \\ \times 9 \\ \hline \end{array}$	$\begin{array}{r} 3 \\ \times 5 \\ \hline \end{array}$	$\begin{array}{r} 9 \\ \times 2 \\ \hline \end{array}$	$\begin{array}{r} 8 \\ \times 8 \\ \hline \end{array}$	$\begin{array}{r} 11 \\ \times 4 \\ \hline \end{array}$
E	$12\overline{)120}$	$9\overline{)18}$	$6\overline{)72}$	$3\overline{)18}$	$8\overline{)80}$	$6\overline{)60}$
F	$2\overline{)18}$	$5\overline{)60}$	$6\overline{)18}$	$8\overline{)56}$	$10\overline{)20}$	$12\overline{)84}$
G	$9\overline{)45}$	$7\overline{)49}$	$12\overline{)108}$	$7\overline{)14}$	$4\overline{)24}$	$6\overline{)42}$

Daily Facts Practice

A	$\begin{array}{r} 4 \\ \times 6 \\ \hline \end{array}$	$12\overline{)72}$	$\begin{array}{r} 9 \\ \times 5 \\ \hline \end{array}$	$10\overline{)0}$	$9\overline{)81}$	$4\overline{)48}$
B	$\begin{array}{r} 2 \\ +9 \\ \hline \end{array}$	$\begin{array}{r} 5 \\ +4 \\ \hline \end{array}$	$\begin{array}{r} 6 \\ +2 \\ \hline \end{array}$	$\begin{array}{r} 8 \\ +6 \\ \hline \end{array}$	$\begin{array}{r} 7 \\ +5 \\ \hline \end{array}$	$\begin{array}{r} 7 \\ +9 \\ \hline \end{array}$
C	$\begin{array}{r} 8 \\ -6 \\ \hline \end{array}$	$\begin{array}{r} 2 \\ +6 \\ \hline \end{array}$	$\begin{array}{r} 6 \\ -2 \\ \hline \end{array}$	$\begin{array}{r} 14 \\ -5 \\ \hline \end{array}$	$\begin{array}{r} 8 \\ +7 \\ \hline \end{array}$	$\begin{array}{r} 10 \\ -7 \\ \hline \end{array}$
D	$\begin{array}{r} 5 \\ +2 \\ \hline \end{array}$	$\begin{array}{r} 7 \\ +4 \\ \hline \end{array}$	$\begin{array}{r} 5 \\ +8 \\ \hline \end{array}$	$\begin{array}{r} 3 \\ +7 \\ \hline \end{array}$	$\begin{array}{r} 6 \\ +3 \\ \hline \end{array}$	$\begin{array}{r} 10 \\ +9 \\ \hline \end{array}$
E	$\begin{array}{r} 15 \\ -10 \\ \hline \end{array}$	$\begin{array}{r} 11 \\ -8 \\ \hline \end{array}$	$\begin{array}{r} 5 \\ -3 \\ \hline \end{array}$	$\begin{array}{r} 8 \\ -5 \\ \hline \end{array}$	$\begin{array}{r} 14 \\ -9 \\ \hline \end{array}$	$\begin{array}{r} 9 \\ -3 \\ \hline \end{array}$
F	$\begin{array}{r} 3 \\ +5 \\ \hline \end{array}$	$\begin{array}{r} 13 \\ -7 \\ \hline \end{array}$	$\begin{array}{r} 6 \\ -3 \\ \hline \end{array}$	$\begin{array}{r} 9 \\ +5 \\ \hline \end{array}$	$\begin{array}{r} 10 \\ -4 \\ \hline \end{array}$	$\begin{array}{r} 14 \\ -6 \\ \hline \end{array}$
G	$\begin{array}{r} 6 \\ \times 0 \\ \hline \end{array}$	$\begin{array}{r} 5 \\ \times 2 \\ \hline \end{array}$	$\begin{array}{r} 5 \\ \times 5 \\ \hline \end{array}$	$\begin{array}{r} 7 \\ \times 6 \\ \hline \end{array}$	$\begin{array}{r} 7 \\ \times 8 \\ \hline \end{array}$	$\begin{array}{r} 8 \\ \times 12 \\ \hline \end{array}$

Daily Facts Practice

A	7×11	12×12	4×9	5×7	8×6	5×4

B	$7)\overline{35}$	$8)\overline{32}$	$9)\overline{108}$	$10)\overline{10}$	$11)\overline{121}$	$12)\overline{144}$

C	$8)\overline{40}$	$8)\overline{72}$	$4)\overline{16}$	$3)\overline{36}$	$12)\overline{132}$	$5)\overline{40}$

D	6×9	4×7	12×5	$12)\overline{60}$	$5)\overline{20}$	$7)\overline{28}$

E	$2 + 7$	$4 + 4$	$6 + 10$	$8 + 9$	$3 + 8$	$5 + 6$

F	$8 - 4$	$9 - 5$	$14 - 7$	$17 - 8$	$9 - 2$	$18 - 10$

G	$5 + 9$	$7 + 7$	$10 + 4$	$16 - 8$	$12 - 6$	$6 - 3$

Daily Facts Practice

A	$\begin{array}{r} 9 \\ \times 12 \\ \hline \end{array}$	$\begin{array}{r} 6 \\ \times 5 \\ \hline \end{array}$	$\begin{array}{r} 3 \\ \times 7 \\ \hline \end{array}$	$\begin{array}{r} 11 \\ \times 11 \\ \hline \end{array}$	$\begin{array}{r} 4 \\ \times 3 \\ \hline \end{array}$	$\begin{array}{r} 4 \\ \times 8 \\ \hline \end{array}$
B	$8\overline{)80}$	$6\overline{)12}$	$12\overline{)36}$	$9\overline{)63}$	$4\overline{)44}$	$8\overline{)72}$
C	$\begin{array}{r} 6 \\ \times 4 \\ \hline \end{array}$	$7\overline{)84}$	$\begin{array}{r} 9 \\ \times 3 \\ \hline \end{array}$	$3\overline{)12}$	$\begin{array}{r} 6 \\ \times 7 \\ \hline \end{array}$	$7\overline{)49}$
D	$\begin{array}{r} 3 \\ \times 9 \\ \hline \end{array}$	$\begin{array}{r} 5 \\ \times 8 \\ \hline \end{array}$	$\begin{array}{r} 4 \\ \times 6 \\ \hline \end{array}$	$\begin{array}{r} 11 \\ \times 12 \\ \hline \end{array}$	$\begin{array}{r} 8 \\ \times 4 \\ \hline \end{array}$	$\begin{array}{r} 9 \\ \times 5 \\ \hline \end{array}$
E	$\begin{array}{r} 5 \\ \times 11 \\ \hline \end{array}$	$\begin{array}{r} 10 \\ \times 9 \\ \hline \end{array}$	$\begin{array}{r} 7 \\ \times 7 \\ \hline \end{array}$	$\begin{array}{r} 12 \\ \times 5 \\ \hline \end{array}$	$\begin{array}{r} 6 \\ \times 6 \\ \hline \end{array}$	$\begin{array}{r} 5 \\ \times 3 \\ \hline \end{array}$
F	$8\overline{)64}$	$5\overline{)55}$	$6\overline{)30}$	$4\overline{)32}$	$2\overline{)24}$	$6\overline{)54}$
G	$5\overline{)25}$	$\begin{array}{r} 3 \\ \times 12 \\ \hline \end{array}$	$7\overline{)21}$	$\begin{array}{r} 8 \\ \times 2 \\ \hline \end{array}$	$12\overline{)96}$	$\begin{array}{r} 8 \\ \times 9 \\ \hline \end{array}$

Daily Facts Practice

A	8 +8	4 +10	7 +6	4 +5	3 +4	9 +3
B	17 −9	12 −5	7 −7	13 −4	8 −2	13 −8
C	3 +9	6 +6	2 +5	7 +3	6 +7	4 +8
D	11 −9	7 −6	10 −3	10 −6	15 −8	8 −4
E	6)24	9)27	7)77	6)42	4)36	2)18
F	12)24	8)32	3)27	2)20	8)24	5)45
G	4 ×4	8 ×3	2)12	4)28	6 ×12	9)99

Daily Facts Practice

A	12 $\times 7$	5 $\times 9$	7 $\times 4$	5 $\times 5$	8 $\times 11$	6 $\times 3$
B	10 $\times 0$	3 $\times 4$	12 $\times 11$	4 $\times 5$	5 $\times 6$	9 $\times 6$
C	$5\overline{)20}$	3 $\times 8$	$9\overline{)81}$	$12\overline{)0}$	2 $\times 12$	$8\overline{)56}$
D	3 $+2$	9 $+4$	6 $+5$	5 $+3$	8 $+4$	6 $+1$
E	16 -9	11 -7	15 -6	9 -8	10 -2	13 -9
F	9 -4	8 -6	5 $+7$	16 -7	9 $+9$	13 -5
G	7 $\times 12$	6 $\times 2$	2 $\times 9$	8 $\times 5$	12 $\times 8$	7 $\times 9$

Daily Facts Practice

A	6×8	2×7	3×5	9×4	12×6	9×8
B	$7\overline{)14}$	$9\overline{)54}$	$6\overline{)66}$	$5\overline{)35}$	$3\overline{)24}$	$7\overline{)63}$
C	$2\overline{)8}$	$4\overline{)24}$	$9\overline{)36}$	$10\overline{)110}$	$6\overline{)72}$	$7\overline{)0}$
D	$9\overline{)45}$	$8\overline{)16}$	$4\overline{)20}$	$12\overline{)72}$	$3\overline{)36}$	$4\overline{)40}$
E	7×5	$8\overline{)40}$	12×1	$5\overline{)30}$	8×7	$7\overline{)70}$
F	$9 +8$	$6 +9$	$8 +5$	$7 +8$	$4 +9$	$4 +7$
G	$18 -9$	$13 -6$	$12 -4$	$11 -2$	$12 -9$	$14 -8$

Daily Facts Practice

A	6 +8	4 +6	8 +3	15 −7	11 −4	12 −7

B	2 ×8	6 ×12	9 ×9	3 ×6	9 ×7	5 ×4

C	6 ×10	3 ×12	0 ×11	6)48	9)72	7)42

$$\begin{array}{r} 0 \\ \times\,0 \\ \hline \end{array}$$

$$\begin{array}{r} 1 \\ \times\,0 \\ \hline \end{array}$$

$$\begin{array}{r} 2 \\ \times\,0 \\ \hline \end{array}$$

$$\begin{array}{r} 3 \\ \times\,0 \\ \hline \end{array}$$

$$\begin{array}{r} 4 \\ \times\,0 \\ \hline \end{array}$$

$$\begin{array}{r} 5 \\ \times\,0 \\ \hline \end{array}$$

$$\begin{array}{r} 6 \\ \times\,0 \\ \hline \end{array}$$

$$\begin{array}{r} 7 \\ \times\,0 \\ \hline \end{array}$$

$$\begin{array}{r} 8 \\ \times\,0 \\ \hline \end{array}$$

$$9 \times 0$$

$$10 \times 0$$

$$11 \times 0$$

$$12 \times 0$$

$$0 \times 1$$

$$1 \times 1$$

$$2 \times 1$$

$$3 \times 1$$

$$4 \times 1$$

$$
\begin{array}{r} 5 \\ \times\,1 \\ \hline \end{array}
\qquad
\begin{array}{r} 6 \\ \times\,1 \\ \hline \end{array}
\qquad
\begin{array}{r} 7 \\ \times\,1 \\ \hline \end{array}
$$

$$
\begin{array}{r} 8 \\ \times\,1 \\ \hline \end{array}
\qquad
\begin{array}{r} 9 \\ \times\,1 \\ \hline \end{array}
\qquad
\begin{array}{r} 10 \\ \times\,1 \\ \hline \end{array}
$$

$$
\begin{array}{r} 11 \\ \times\,1 \\ \hline \end{array}
\qquad
\begin{array}{r} 12 \\ \times\,1 \\ \hline \end{array}
\qquad
\begin{array}{r} 0 \\ \times\,2 \\ \hline \end{array}
$$

$$\begin{array}{r} 1 \\ \times 2 \\ \hline \end{array}$$

$$\begin{array}{r} 2 \\ \times 2 \\ \hline \end{array}$$

$$\begin{array}{r} 3 \\ \times 2 \\ \hline \end{array}$$

$$\begin{array}{r} 4 \\ \times 2 \\ \hline \end{array}$$

$$\begin{array}{r} 5 \\ \times 2 \\ \hline \end{array}$$

$$\begin{array}{r} 6 \\ \times 2 \\ \hline \end{array}$$

$$\begin{array}{r} 7 \\ \times 2 \\ \hline \end{array}$$

$$\begin{array}{r} 8 \\ \times 2 \\ \hline \end{array}$$

$$\begin{array}{r} 9 \\ \times 2 \\ \hline \end{array}$$

$$\begin{array}{r} 10 \\ \times 2 \\ \hline \end{array}$$

$$\begin{array}{r} 11 \\ \times 2 \\ \hline \end{array}$$

$$\begin{array}{r} 12 \\ \times 2 \\ \hline \end{array}$$

$$\begin{array}{r} 0 \\ \times 3 \\ \hline \end{array}$$

$$\begin{array}{r} 1 \\ \times 3 \\ \hline \end{array}$$

$$\begin{array}{r} 2 \\ \times 3 \\ \hline \end{array}$$

$$\begin{array}{r} 3 \\ \times 3 \\ \hline \end{array}$$

$$\begin{array}{r} 4 \\ \times 3 \\ \hline \end{array}$$

$$\begin{array}{r} 5 \\ \times 3 \\ \hline \end{array}$$

6 ×3	7 ×3	8 ×3
9 ×3	10 ×3	11 ×3
12 ×3	0 ×4	1 ×4

$$\begin{array}{r} 2 \\ \times\,4 \\ \hline \end{array}$$

$$\begin{array}{r} 3 \\ \times\,4 \\ \hline \end{array}$$

$$\begin{array}{r} 4 \\ \times\,4 \\ \hline \end{array}$$

$$\begin{array}{r} 5 \\ \times\,4 \\ \hline \end{array}$$

$$\begin{array}{r} 6 \\ \times\,4 \\ \hline \end{array}$$

$$\begin{array}{r} 7 \\ \times\,4 \\ \hline \end{array}$$

$$\begin{array}{r} 8 \\ \times\,4 \\ \hline \end{array}$$

$$\begin{array}{r} 9 \\ \times\,4 \\ \hline \end{array}$$

$$\begin{array}{r} 10 \\ \times\,4 \\ \hline \end{array}$$

11	12	0
×4	×4	×5

1	2	3
×5	×5	×5

4	5	6
×5	×5	×5

$$\begin{array}{r} 7 \\ \times 5 \\ \hline \end{array}$$
$$\begin{array}{r} 8 \\ \times 5 \\ \hline \end{array}$$
$$\begin{array}{r} 9 \\ \times 5 \\ \hline \end{array}$$

$$\begin{array}{r} 10 \\ \times 5 \\ \hline \end{array}$$
$$\begin{array}{r} 11 \\ \times 6 \\ \hline \end{array}$$
$$\begin{array}{r} 12 \\ \times 5 \\ \hline \end{array}$$

$$\begin{array}{r} 0 \\ \times 6 \\ \hline \end{array}$$
$$\begin{array}{r} 1 \\ \times 6 \\ \hline \end{array}$$
$$\begin{array}{r} 2 \\ \times 6 \\ \hline \end{array}$$

3 ×6	4 ×6	5 ×6
6 ×6	7 ×6	8 ×6
9 ×6	10 ×6	11 ×6

© Harcourt

$$\begin{array}{r} 12 \\ \times\,6 \\ \hline \end{array}$$

$$\begin{array}{r} 0 \\ \times\,7 \\ \hline \end{array}$$

$$\begin{array}{r} 1 \\ \times\,7 \\ \hline \end{array}$$

$$\begin{array}{r} 2 \\ \times\,7 \\ \hline \end{array}$$

$$\begin{array}{r} 3 \\ \times\,7 \\ \hline \end{array}$$

$$\begin{array}{r} 4 \\ \times\,7 \\ \hline \end{array}$$

$$\begin{array}{r} 5 \\ \times\,7 \\ \hline \end{array}$$

$$\begin{array}{r} 6 \\ \times\,7 \\ \hline \end{array}$$

$$\begin{array}{r} 7 \\ \times\,7 \\ \hline \end{array}$$

8	9	10
×7	×7	×7

11	12	0
×7	×7	×8

1	2	3
×8	×8	×8

© Harcourt

$$
\begin{array}{r}
4 \\
\times 8 \\
\hline
\end{array}
\qquad
\begin{array}{r}
5 \\
\times 8 \\
\hline
\end{array}
\qquad
\begin{array}{r}
6 \\
\times 8 \\
\hline
\end{array}
$$

$$
\begin{array}{r}
7 \\
\times 8 \\
\hline
\end{array}
\qquad
\begin{array}{r}
8 \\
\times 8 \\
\hline
\end{array}
\qquad
\begin{array}{r}
9 \\
\times 8 \\
\hline
\end{array}
$$

$$
\begin{array}{r}
10 \\
\times 8 \\
\hline
\end{array}
\qquad
\begin{array}{r}
11 \\
\times 8 \\
\hline
\end{array}
\qquad
\begin{array}{r}
12 \\
\times 8 \\
\hline
\end{array}
$$

$$\begin{array}{r} 0 \\ \times\,9 \\ \hline \end{array}$$

$$\begin{array}{r} 1 \\ \times\,9 \\ \hline \end{array}$$

$$\begin{array}{r} 2 \\ \times\,9 \\ \hline \end{array}$$

$$\begin{array}{r} 3 \\ \times\,9 \\ \hline \end{array}$$

$$\begin{array}{r} 4 \\ \times\,9 \\ \hline \end{array}$$

$$\begin{array}{r} 5 \\ \times\,9 \\ \hline \end{array}$$

$$\begin{array}{r} 6 \\ \times\,9 \\ \hline \end{array}$$

$$\begin{array}{r} 7 \\ \times\,9 \\ \hline \end{array}$$

$$\begin{array}{r} 8 \\ \times\,9 \\ \hline \end{array}$$

$\begin{array}{r}9\\ \times 9\\ \hline\end{array}$	$\begin{array}{r}10\\ \times 9\\ \hline\end{array}$	$\begin{array}{r}11\\ \times 9\\ \hline\end{array}$
$\begin{array}{r}12\\ \times 9\\ \hline\end{array}$	$\begin{array}{r}0\\ \times 10\\ \hline\end{array}$	$\begin{array}{r}1\\ \times 10\\ \hline\end{array}$
$\begin{array}{r}2\\ \times 10\\ \hline\end{array}$	$\begin{array}{r}3\\ \times 10\\ \hline\end{array}$	$\begin{array}{r}4\\ \times 10\\ \hline\end{array}$

© Harcourt

Fact Cards

$$\begin{array}{r} 5 \\ \times\,10 \\ \hline \end{array}$$

$$\begin{array}{r} 6 \\ \times\,10 \\ \hline \end{array}$$

$$\begin{array}{r} 7 \\ \times\,10 \\ \hline \end{array}$$

$$\begin{array}{r} 8 \\ \times\,10 \\ \hline \end{array}$$

$$\begin{array}{r} 9 \\ \times\,10 \\ \hline \end{array}$$

$$\begin{array}{r} 10 \\ \times\,10 \\ \hline \end{array}$$

$$\begin{array}{r} 11 \\ \times\,10 \\ \hline \end{array}$$

$$\begin{array}{r} 12 \\ \times\,10 \\ \hline \end{array}$$

$$\begin{array}{r} 0 \\ \times\,11 \\ \hline \end{array}$$

$$\begin{array}{r} 1 \\ \times\, 11 \\ \hline \end{array}$$

$$\begin{array}{r} 2 \\ \times\, 11 \\ \hline \end{array}$$

$$\begin{array}{r} 3 \\ \times\, 11 \\ \hline \end{array}$$

$$\begin{array}{r} 4 \\ \times\, 11 \\ \hline \end{array}$$

$$\begin{array}{r} 5 \\ \times\, 11 \\ \hline \end{array}$$

$$\begin{array}{r} 6 \\ \times\, 11 \\ \hline \end{array}$$

$$\begin{array}{r} 7 \\ \times\, 11 \\ \hline \end{array}$$

$$\begin{array}{r} 8 \\ \times\, 11 \\ \hline \end{array}$$

$$\begin{array}{r} 9 \\ \times\, 11 \\ \hline \end{array}$$

$\begin{array}{r} 10 \\ \times 11 \\ \hline \end{array}$	$\begin{array}{r} 11 \\ \times 11 \\ \hline \end{array}$	$\begin{array}{r} 12 \\ \times 11 \\ \hline \end{array}$
$\begin{array}{r} 0 \\ \times 12 \\ \hline \end{array}$	$\begin{array}{r} 1 \\ \times 12 \\ \hline \end{array}$	$\begin{array}{r} 2 \\ \times 12 \\ \hline \end{array}$
$\begin{array}{r} 3 \\ \times 12 \\ \hline \end{array}$	$\begin{array}{r} 4 \\ \times 12 \\ \hline \end{array}$	$\begin{array}{r} 5 \\ \times 12 \\ \hline \end{array}$

$$\begin{array}{r} 6 \\ \times 12 \\ \hline \end{array}$$

$$\begin{array}{r} 7 \\ \times 12 \\ \hline \end{array}$$

$$\begin{array}{r} 8 \\ \times 12 \\ \hline \end{array}$$

$$\begin{array}{r} 9 \\ \times 12 \\ \hline \end{array}$$

$$\begin{array}{r} 10 \\ \times 12 \\ \hline \end{array}$$

$$\begin{array}{r} 11 \\ \times 12 \\ \hline \end{array}$$

$$\begin{array}{r} 12 \\ \times 12 \\ \hline \end{array}$$

$1\overline{)2}$

$1\overline{)5}$

$1\overline{)8}$

$1\overline{)1}$

$1\overline{)4}$

$1\overline{)7}$

$1\overline{)0}$

$1\overline{)3}$

$1\overline{)6}$

$1\overline{)11}$

$2\overline{)2}$

$2\overline{)8}$

$1\overline{)10}$

$2\overline{)0}$

$2\overline{)6}$

$1\overline{)9}$

$1\overline{)12}$

$2\overline{)4}$

$2\overline{)14}$ $2\overline{)20}$ $3\overline{)0}$

$2\overline{)12}$ $2\overline{)18}$ $2\overline{)24}$

$2\overline{)10}$ $2\overline{)16}$ $2\overline{)22}$

$3\overline{)9}$

$3\overline{)18}$

$3\overline{)27}$

$3\overline{)6}$

$3\overline{)15}$

$3\overline{)24}$

$3\overline{)3}$

$3\overline{)12}$

$3\overline{)21}$

Fact Cards

$3\overline{)36}$

$4\overline{)8}$

$4\overline{)20}$

$3\overline{)33}$

$4\overline{)4}$

$4\overline{)16}$

$3\overline{)30}$

$4\overline{)0}$

$4\overline{)12}$

© Harcourt

$4\overline{)32}$

$4\overline{)44}$

$5\overline{)5}$

$4\overline{)28}$

$4\overline{)40}$

$5\overline{)0}$

$4\overline{)24}$

$4\overline{)36}$

$4\overline{)48}$

$5 \overline{)20}$

$5 \overline{)35}$

$5 \overline{)50}$

$5 \overline{)15}$

$5 \overline{)30}$

$5 \overline{)45}$

$5 \overline{)10}$

$5 \overline{)25}$

$5 \overline{)40}$

© Harcourt

$6\overline{)0}$

$6\overline{)18}$

$6\overline{)36}$

$5\overline{)60}$

$6\overline{)12}$

$6\overline{)30}$

$5\overline{)55}$

$6\overline{)6}$

$6\overline{)24}$

6)54   6)72   7)14

6)48   6)66   7)7

6)42   6)60   7)0

$7\overline{)35}$

$7\overline{)56}$

$7\overline{)77}$

$7\overline{)28}$

$7\overline{)49}$

$7\overline{)70}$

$7\overline{)21}$

$7\overline{)42}$

$7\overline{)63}$

Fact Cards

8)8

8)32

8)56

8)0

8)24

8)48

7)84

8)16

8)40

$8\overline{)80}$

$9\overline{)0}$

$9\overline{)27}$

$8\overline{)72}$

$8\overline{)96}$

$9\overline{)18}$

$8\overline{)64}$

$8\overline{)88}$

$9\overline{)9}$

Fact Cards

$9\overline{)54}$

$9\overline{)81}$

$9\overline{)108}$

$9\overline{)45}$

$9\overline{)72}$

$9\overline{)99}$

$9\overline{)36}$

$9\overline{)63}$

$9\overline{)90}$

Fact Cards

$10\overline{)20}$

$10\overline{)50}$

$10\overline{)80}$

$10\overline{)10}$

$10\overline{)40}$

$10\overline{)70}$

$10\overline{)0}$

$10\overline{)30}$

$10\overline{)60}$

Fact Cards

$10\overline{)110}$

$11\overline{)11}$

$11\overline{)44}$

$10\overline{)100}$

$11\overline{)0}$

$11\overline{)33}$

$10\overline{)90}$

$10\overline{)120}$

$11\overline{)22}$

$11\overline{)77}$

$11\overline{)110}$

$12\overline{)0}$

$11\overline{)66}$

$11\overline{)99}$

$11\overline{)132}$

$11\overline{)55}$

$11\overline{)88}$

$11\overline{)121}$

$12\overline{)36}$

$12\overline{)72}$

$12\overline{)108}$

$12\overline{)24}$

$12\overline{)60}$

$12\overline{)96}$

$12\overline{)12}$

$12\overline{)48}$

$12\overline{)84}$

$12\overline{)144}$

$12\overline{)132}$

$12\overline{)120}$

VOCABULARY CARDS

Use the vocabulary cards to practice and review this year's new math terms. Suggestions for using the cards are in the *Teacher's Edition,* on the Vocabulary Power page.

Consider having students organize their vocabulary cards in Math Word Files—containers made from zip-top bags or small boxes, such as crayon or computer disk boxes. Encourage students to consult their Math Word Files to confirm meanings, verify pronunciations, and check spellings.

To copy, set your machine to 2-sided copies. Align the perforated edge with the left-hand (or top) guide on the glass and copy. Flip the page, align the perforated edge with the opposite (right-hand or bottom) guide, and copy.

Pronunciation Key

a	add, map	h	hope, hate	ô	order, jaw	th	this, bathe
ā	ace, rate	i	it, give	oi	oil, boy	u	up, done
â(r)	care, air	ī	ice, write	ou	pout, now	û(r)	burn, term
ä	palm, father	j	joy, ledge	o͝o	took, full	yo͞o	fuse, few
b	bat, rub	k	cool, take	o͞o	pool, food	v	vain, eve
ch	check, catch	l	look, rule	p	pit, stop	w	win, away
d	dog, rod	m	move, seem	r	run, poor	y	yet, yearn
e	end, pet	n	nice, tin	s	see, pass	z	zest, muse
ē	equal, tree	ng	ring, song	sh	sure, rush	zh	vision,
f	fit, half	o	odd, hot	t	talk, sit		pleasure
g	go, log	ō	open, so	th	thin, both		

ə   the schwa, an unstressed vowel representing the sound spelled *a* in above, *e* in sicken, *i* in possible, *o* in melon, *u* in circus

Other symbols:
• separates words into syllables
′ indicates stress on a syllable

period	expression
millions	variable
benchmark	Commutative Property of Addition
round	Associative Property of Addition

ik•spre′shən
A part of a number sentence that combines numbers and operation signs but does not have an equal sign

Chapter 4, Lesson 1

pir′ē•əd
Each group of three digits separated by commas in a multidigit number

Chapter 1, Lesson 2

vâr′ē•ə•bəl
A letter or symbol that stands for a number or numbers

Chapter 4, Lesson 1

mil′yənz
The period after thousands

Chapter 1, Lesson 3

kə•myōō′tə•tiv prä′pər•tē əv ə•di′shən
The property that states that when the order of two addends is changed, the sum is the same

Chapter 4, Lesson 2

bench′märk
A known number of things that helps you understand the size or amount of a different number of things

Chapter 1, Lesson 4

ə•sō′shē•ə•tiv prä′pər•tē əv ə•di′shən
The property that states that you can group addends in different ways and still get the same sum

Chapter 4, Lesson 2

round
To replace a number with another number that tells about how many or how much

Chapter 2, Lesson 4

Identity Property of Addition	**century**
equation	**decade**
second	**survey**
elapsed time	**frequency**

sen′chə•rē
**A measure of time equal to
100 years**

Chapter 5, Lesson 4

ī•den′tə•tē prä′pər•tē əv ə•di′shən
**The property that states
that when you add zero
to any number, the sum
is that number**

Chapter 4, Lesson 2

de′kād
**A measure of time equal to
10 years**

Chapter 5, Lesson 4

i•kwā′zhən
**A number sentence which
shows that two quantities
are equal**

Chapter 4, Lesson 3

sûr′vā
**A method of gathering
information to record data**

Chapter 6, Lesson 1

se′kənd
**A small unit of time;
60 seconds = 1 minute**

Chapter 5, Lesson 1

frē′kwen•sē
**The number of times an
event occurs**

Chapter 6, Lesson 1

i•lapst′ tīm
**The time that passes from
the start of an activity to the
end of that activity**

Chapter 5, Lesson 2

cumulative frequency	line plot
mean	range
median	outlier
mode	stem-and-leaf plot

līn plät
A graph that shows the frequency of data along a number line

Chapter 6, Lesson 3

kyōō′myə•lə•tiv frē′kwen•sē
A running total of items being counted

Chapter 6, Lesson 1

rānj
The difference between the greatest number and the least number in a set of data

Chapter 6, Lesson 3

mēn
The number found by dividing the sum of the set of numbers by the number of addends

Chapter 6, Lesson 2

out′lī•ər
A value separated from the rest of the data

Chapter 6, Lesson 3

mē′dē•ən
The middle number in an ordered set of data

Chapter 6, Lesson 2

stem ənd lēf plät
A data display that shows groups of data arranged by place value

Chapter 6, Lesson 4

mōd
The number(s) or item(s) that occur most often in a set of data

Chapter 6, Lesson 2

stem	double-bar graph
leaf	trends
scale	line graph
interval	circle graph

du′bəl bär graf
A graph used to compare similar kinds of data

Chapter 7, Lesson 1

stem
A tens digit in a stem-and-leaf plot

Chapter 6, Lesson 4

trendz
On a graph, areas where the data increase, decrease, or stay the same over time

Chapter 7, Lesson 2

lēf
A ones digit in a stem-and-leaf plot

Chapter 6, Lesson 4

līn graf
A graph that uses a line to show how data change over a period of time

Chapter 7, Lesson 2

skāl
The numbers placed at fixed distances on a graph to help label the graph

Chapter 6, Lesson 5

sûr′kəl graf
A graph in the shape of a circle that shows data as a whole made up of different parts

Chapter 7, Lesson 4

in′tər•vəl
The difference between two numbers on the scale of a graph

Chapter 6, Lesson 5

inverse operations	Zero Property of Multiplication
fact family	Commutative Property of Multiplication
multiple	Associative Property of Multiplication
Identity Property of Multiplication	order of operations

zir´ō prä´pər•tē əv
mul•tə•plə•kā´shən

The property that states that the product of 0 and any number is 0

Chapter 8, Lesson 5

in´vərs ä•pə•rā´shənz

Opposite operations that undo each other, such as addition and subtraction or multiplication and division

Chapter 8, Lesson 1

kə•myōō´tə•tiv prä´pər•tē əv
mul•tə•plə•kā´shən

The property that states that when the order of two factors is changed, the product is the same

Chapter 8, Lesson 5

fakt fam´ə•lē

A set of related multiplication and division or addition and subtraction equations

Chapter 8, Lesson 1

ə•sō´shē•ə•tiv prä´pər•tē əv
mul•tə•plə•kā´shən

The property that states that you can group factors in different ways and still get the same product

Chapter 8, Lesson 5

mul´tə•pəl

The product of a given whole number and another whole number

Chapter 8, Lesson 4

ôr´dər əv ä•pə•rā´shənz

Rules for performing operations in expressions with more than one operation; do the operations inside parentheses, then multiply and divide from left to right, then add and subtract from left to right

Chapter 9, Lesson 2

ī•den´tə•tē prä´pər•tē əv
mul•tə•plə•kā´shən

The property that states that the product of any number and 1 is that number

Chapter 8, Lesson 5

Vocabulary Cards

compatible numbers	divisible
Distributive Property	prime number
multistep problem	composite number
remainder	square number

də•vi′zi•bəl

Capable of being divided so that the quotient is a whole number and the remainder is zero

Chapter 16, Lesson 1

kəm•pa′tə•bəl nəm′bərz

Numbers that are easy to compute mentally

Chapter 10, Lesson 2

prīm num′bər

A number that has only two factors: 1 and itself

Chapter 16, Lesson 3

di•strib′yə•tiv prä′pər•tē

The property that states that multiplying a sum by a number is the same as multiplying each addend by the number and then adding the products

Chapter 11, Lesson 2

kəm•pä′zət num′bər

A whole number that has more than two factors

Chapter 16, Lesson 3

mul′tē•step prä′bləm

A problem requiring more than one step to solve

Chapter 12, Lesson 5

skwâr num′bər

The product of a number and itself

Chapter 16, Lesson 5

ri•mān′dər

The amount left over when a number cannot be divided evenly

Chapter 13, Lesson 1

© Harcourt

square root	**ray**
point	**plane**
line	**angle**
line segment	**vertex**

rā
A part of a line that has one endpoint and continues without end in one direction

Chapter 17, Lesson 1

skwâr ro͞ot
One of two equal factors of a number

Chapter 16, Lesson 5

plān
A flat surface that extends without end in all directions

Chapter 17, Lesson 1

point
An exact location in space

Chapter 17, Lesson 1

ang′gəl
A figure formed by two line segments or rays that share the same endpoint

Chapter 17, Lesson 2

līn
A straight path of points in a plane that continues without end in both directions with no endpoints

Chapter 17, Lesson 1

vûr′teks
The point at which two rays of an angle or two or more line segments meet in a plane figure

Chapter 17, Lesson 2

līn seg′mənt
A part of a line that includes two points called endpoints and all the points between them

Chapter 17, Lesson 1

© Harcourt

protractor	obtuse angle
degree (°)	straight angle
right angle	intersecting lines
acute angle	parallel lines

ab•tōōs′ ang′gəl
An angle that has a measure greater than 90° and less than 180°

Chapter 17, Lesson 2

prō•trak′tər
A tool for measuring the size of an angle

Chapter 17, Lesson 2

strāt ang′gəl
An angle that has a measure of 180°

Chapter 17, Lesson 2

di•grē′
A unit for measuring angles or temperatures

Chapter 17, Lesson 2

in•tər•sek′ting līnz
Lines that cross each other at exactly one point

Chapter 17, Lesson 3

rīt ang′gəl
An angle that forms a square corner and has a measure of 90°

Chapter 17, Lesson 2

par′ə•lel līnz
Lines in the same plane that never intersect and are always the same distance apart

Chapter 17, Lesson 3

ə•kyōōt′ ang′gəl
An angle that has a measure greater than 0° and less than 90°

Chapter 17, Lesson 2

Vocabulary Cards

perpendicular lines	quadrilateral
polygon	pentagon
regular polygon	hexagon
triangle	octagon

kwä•drə•la′tə•rəl
A polygon with four sides

Chapter 18, Lesson 1

pər•pən•dik′yə•lər līnz
Two lines that intersect to form four right angles

Chapter 17, Lesson 3

pen′tə•gän
A polygon with five sides

Chapter 18, Lesson 1

pä′lē•gän
A closed plane figure with straight sides, each of which is a line segment

Chapter 18, Lesson 1

hek′sə•gän
A polygon with six sides

Chapter 18, Lesson 1

reg′yə•lər pä′lē•gän
A polygon whose sides are all the same length

Chapter 18, Lesson 1

äk′tə•gän
A polygon with eight sides

Chapter 18, Lesson 1

trī′ang•gəl
A polygon with three sides

Chapter 18, Lesson 1

equilateral triangle	acute triangle
isosceles triangle	obtuse triangle
scalene triangle	parallelogram
right triangle	rhombus

ə•kyo͞ot′ trī′ang•gəl
A triangle with three acute angles

ē•kwə•la′tə•rəl trī′ang•gəl
A triangle with three equal, or congruent, sides

əb•to͞os′ trī′ang•gəl
A triangle with one obtuse angle

ī•sä′sə•lēz trī′ang•gəl
A triangle with two equal, or congruent, sides

par•ə•lel′ə•gram
A quadrilateral whose opposite sides are parallel and equal, or congruent

skā′lēn trī′ang•gəl
A triangle with no equal, or congruent, sides

räm′bəs
A parallelogram with four equal, or congruent, sides

rīt trī′ang•gəl
A triangle with one right angle

© Harcourt

Vocabulary Cards

trapezoid	chord
Venn diagram	**diameter**
circle	radius
center	compass

kôrd

A line segment that has endpoints on a circle

Chapter 18, Lesson 5

tra′pə•zoid

A quadrilateral with exactly one pair of parallel sides

Chapter 18, Lesson 3

dī•am′ə•tər

A line segment that passes through the center of a circle and has endpoints on the circle

Chapter 18, Lesson 5

ven dī′ə•gram

A diagram that shows relationships among sets of things

Chapter 18, Lesson 4

rā′dē•əs

A line segment that has one endpoint at the center of a circle and the other endpoint on the circle

Chapter 18, Lesson 5

sûr′kəl

A closed figure made up of points that are all the same distance from the center

Chapter 18, Lesson 5

kum′pəs

A tool used to construct circles

Chapter 18, Lesson 5

sen′tər

The point inside a circle that is the same distance from each point on the circle

Chapter 18, Lesson 5

© Harcourt

line symmetry	transformation
rotational symmetry	translation
congruent	reflection
similar	rotation

Vocabulary Cards

trans•fər•mā′shən

A movement of a figure to a new position by a translation, reflection, or rotation

Chapter 19, Lesson 4

līn si′mə•trē

What a figure has if it can be folded about a line so that its two parts match exactly

Chapter 19, Lesson 1

trans•lā′shən

A movement of a figure to a new position along a straight line

Chapter 19, Lesson 4

rō•tā′shən•əl si′mə•trē

What a figure has if it can be turned about a central point and still look the same in at least two positions

Chapter 19, Lesson 1

rē•flek′shən

A movement of a figure to a new position by flipping the figure over a line

Chapter 19, Lesson 4

kən•groo′ənt

Having the same size and shape

Chapter 19, Lesson 2

rō•tā′shən

A movement of a figure to a new position by rotating the figure around a point

Chapter 19, Lesson 4

si′mə•lər

Having the same shape but possibly different in size

Chapter 19, Lesson 2

Vocabulary Cards

© Harcourt

© Harcourt

tessellation	positive numbers
degree Fahrenheit (°F)	opposites
degree Celsius (°C)	inequality
negative numbers	ordered pair

pä′zə•tiv num′bərz

All numbers to the right of zero on the number line

Chapter 20, Lesson 3

---

tes•ə•lā′shən

A repeating pattern of closed figures that covers a surface with no gaps and no overlaps

Chapter 19, Lesson 5

ä′pə•zəts

Numbers that are the same distance from zero but in opposite directions from zero

Chapter 20, Lesson 3

---

di•grē′ far′ən•hīt

A standard unit for measuring temperature

Chapter 20, Lesson 1

---

in•i•kwol′ə•tē

A mathematical sentence that shows that two expressions do not represent the same quantity

Chapter 20, Lesson 5

---

di•grē′ səl′sē•us

A metric unit for measuring temperature

Chapter 20, Lesson 2

ôr′dərd pâr

A pair of numbers used to locate a point on a coordinate grid; the first number tells how far to move horizontally, and the second number tells how far to move vertically

Chapter 20, Lesson 6

---

ne′gə•tiv num′bərz

All numbers to the left of zero on the number line

Chapter 20, Lesson 3

Vocabulary Cards

x-axis	fraction
y-axis	numerator
x-coordinate	denominator
y-coordinate	equivalent fractions

frak'shən

A number that names part of a whole or part of a group

Chapter 21, Lesson 1

eks ak'səs

The horizontal line on a coordinate grid, or plane

Chapter 20, Lesson 6

noo'mə•rā•tər

The number above the bar in a fraction that tells how many parts of the whole or group are being considered

Chapter 21, Lesson 1

wī ak'səs

The vertical line on a coordinate grid, or plane

Chapter 20, Lesson 6

di•nä'mə•nā•tər

The number below the bar in a fraction that tells how many equal parts are in the whole or group

Chapter 21, Lesson 1

eks kō•ôr'də•nət

The first number in an ordered pair that tells how far to move horizontally

Chapter 20, Lesson 6

ē•kwiv'ə•lənt frak'shənz

Two or more fractions that name the same amount

Chapter 21, Lesson 2

wī kō•ôr'də•nət

The second number in an ordered pair that tells how far to move vertically

Chapter 20, Lesson 6

simplest form	outcome
mixed number	event
like fractions	predict
unlike fractions	likely

out'kum
A possible result of an experiment

Chapter 23, Lesson 1

sim'pləst fôrm
The state a fraction is in when 1 is the only number that can divide evenly into both the numerator and the denominator

Chapter 21, Lesson 2

i•vent'
One outcome or a combination of outcomes in an experiment

Chapter 23, Lesson 1

mikst num'bər
An amount given as a whole number and a fraction

Chapter 21, Lesson 5

pri•dikt'
To make a reasonable guess about what will happen

Chapter 23, Lesson 1

līk frak'shənz
Fractions with the same denominator

Chapter 22, Lesson 1

lī'klē
Having a greater than even chance of happening

Chapter 23, Lesson 1

un'līk frak'shənz
Fractions with different denominators

Chapter 22, Lesson 5

Vocabulary Cards

© Harcourt

unlikely	**linear units**
equally likely	**inch (in.)**
mathematical probability	**foot (ft)**
tree diagram	**yard (yd)**

lin′ē•ər yōō′nətz
Units for measuring length, width, height, or distance

Chapter 24, Lesson 1

un•li′klē
Having a less than even chance of happening

Chapter 23, Lesson 1

inch
A customary unit for measuring length or distance; 12 of these are equivalent to 1 foot

Chapter 24, Lesson 1

ē′kwəl•lē li′klē
Having the same chance of happening

Chapter 23, Lesson 1

fŏŏt
A customary unit for measuring length or distance that is equivalent to 12 inches

Chapter 24, Lesson 1

math•ma′ti•kəl prä•bə•bi′lə•tē
A comparison of the number of favorable outcomes to the number of possible outcomes of an event

Chapter 23, Lesson 3

yärd
A customary unit for measuring length or distance that is equivalent to 3 feet

Chapter 24, Lesson 1

trē dī′ə•gram
An organized list that shows all possible outcomes of an event

Chapter 23, Lesson 5

© Harcourt

Vocabulary Cards

mile (mi)	cup (c)
capacity	pint (pt)
teaspoon (tsp)	quart (qt)
tablespoon (tbsp)	gallon (gal)

kup
A customary unit for measuring capacity that is equivalent to 8 ounces

Chapter 24, Lesson 4

mīl
A customary unit for measuring length or distance that is equivalent to 5,280 feet

Chapter 24, Lesson 1

pīnt
A customary unit for measuring capacity that is equivalent to 2 cups

Chapter 24, Lesson 4

kə•pa′sə•tē
The amount a container can hold when filled

Chapter 24, Lesson 4

kwôrt
A customary unit for measuring capacity that is equivalent to 2 pints

Chapter 24, Lesson 4

tē′spo͞on
A customary unit for measuring capacity; 3 of these are equivalent to 1 tablespoon

Chapter 24, Lesson 4

ga′lən
A customary unit for measuring capacity that is equivalent to 4 quarts

Chapter 24, Lesson 4

tā′bəl•spo͞on
A customary unit for measuring capacity that is equivalent to 3 teaspoons

Chapter 24, Lesson 4

Vocabulary Cards

© Harcourt

ounce (oz)	**centimeter (cm)**
pound (lb)	**decimeter (dm)**
ton (T)	**meter (m)**
millimeter (mm)	**kilometer (km)**

sən´tə•mē•tər

A metric unit for measuring length or distance; 100 centimeters = 1 meter

Chapter 25, Lesson 1

ouns

A customary unit for measuring weight; 16 of these are equivalent to 1 pound

Chapter 24, Lesson 5

de´sə•mē•tər

A metric unit for measuring length or distance; 10 decimeters = 1 meter

Chapter 25, Lesson 1

pound

A customary unit for measuring weight that is equivalent to 16 ounces

Chapter 24, Lesson 5

mē´tər

A metric unit for measuring length or distance; 1 meter = 100 centimeters

Chapter 25, Lesson 1

tun

A customary unit for measuring weight that is equivalent to 2,000 pounds

Chapter 24, Lesson 5

kə•lä´mə•tər

A metric unit for measuring length or distance; 1 kilometer = 1,000 meters

Chapter 25, Lesson 1

mi´lə•mē•tər

A metric unit for measuring length or distance; 1,000 millimeters = 1 meter

Chapter 25, Lesson 1

© Harcourt

milliliter (mL)	**kilogram (kg)**
liter (L)	**decimal**
mass	**decimal point**
gram (g)	**thousandth**

kil′ə•gram
A metric unit for measuring mass; 1 kilogram = 1,000 grams

Chapter 25, Lesson 4

mi′lə•lē•tər
A metric unit for measuring capacity; 1,000 milliliters = 1 liter

Chapter 25, Lesson 3

de′sə•məl
A number with one or more digits to the right of the decimal point

Chapter 26, Lesson 1

lē′tər
A metric unit for measuring capacity; 1 liter = 1,000 milliliters

Chapter 25, Lesson 3

de′sə•məl point
A symbol used to separate dollars from cents in money and to separate the ones and the tenths places in a decimal

Chapter 26, Lesson 1

mas
The amount of matter in an object

Chapter 25, Lesson 4

thou′zəndth
One of one thousand equal parts

Chapter 26, Lesson 2

gram
A metric unit for measuring mass; 1,000 grams = 1 kilogram

Chapter 25, Lesson 4

Vocabulary Cards

equivalent decimals	**area**
perimeter	**two-dimensional**
formula	**three-dimensional**
circumference	**triangular prism**

âr′ē•ə
**The number of square units
needed to cover a surface**

Chapter 29, Lesson 1

ē•kwiv′ə•lənt de′sə•məlz
**Two or more decimals that
name the same amount**

Chapter 26, Lesson 3

to͞o də•men′shən•əl
**Measured in two directions,
such as length and width**

Chapter 30, Lesson 1

pə•ri′mə•tər
The distance around a figure

Chapter 28, Lesson 1

thrē də•men′shən•əl
**Measured in three
directions, such as length,
width, and height**

Chapter 30, Lesson 1

fôr′myə•lə
**A set of symbols
that expresses a
mathematical rule**

Chapter 28, Lesson 2

trī•ang′gyə•lər priz′əm
**A solid figure that has two
triangular bases and three
rectangular faces**

Chapter 30, Lesson 1

sər•kum′fər•əns
The distance around a circle

Chapter 28, Lesson 3

© Harcourt

triangular pyramid	net
edge	volume
face	cubic unit
vertex	

net

**A two-dimensional pattern
that can be folded to make a
three-dimensional figure**

Chapter 30, Lesson 2

---

trī•ang′gyə•lər pir′ə•mid

**A pyramid that has a
triangular base and three
triangular faces**

Chapter 30, Lesson 1

---

väl′yəm

**The measure of the
amount of space a solid
figure occupies**

Chapter 30, Lesson 3

---

ej

**The line segment where two
or more faces of a solid
figure meet**

Chapter 30, Lesson 1

---

kyōō′bik yōō′nət

**A unit of volume
with dimensions of
1 unit × 1 unit × 1 unit**

Chapter 30, Lesson 3

---

fās

**A polygon that is a flat
surface of a solid figure**

Chapter 30, Lesson 1

---

vûr′teks

**The point at which two rays
of an angle or two or more
line segments meet in a
plane figure or at which
three or more edges meet
in a solid figure**

Chapter 30, Lesson 1

IT'S IN THE BAG

This section's blackline masters accompany "It's in the Bag."
Directions for these and other fun "It's in the Bag" projects appear
in every unit of your *Harcourt Math* Student and Teacher Editions.

Ring Place-Value Strip

0	1	2	3	4
5	6	7	8	9
0	1	2	3	4
5	6	7	8	9
0	1	2	3	4
5	6	7	8	9
0	1	2	3	4
5	6	7	8	9

Gold Medal Graphing

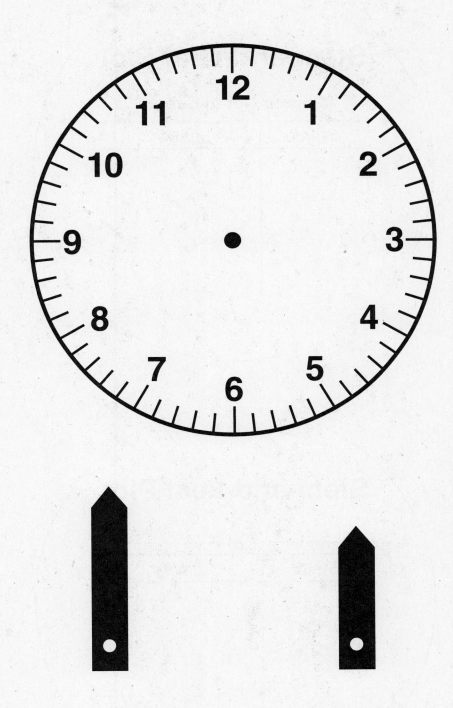

© Harcourt

Gold Medal Graphing

Stem-and-Leaf Plot

Time to Get to School

Stem	Leaves

Stem-and-Leaf Plot

Stem	Leaves

© Harcourt

Gold Medal Graphing

Line Plot

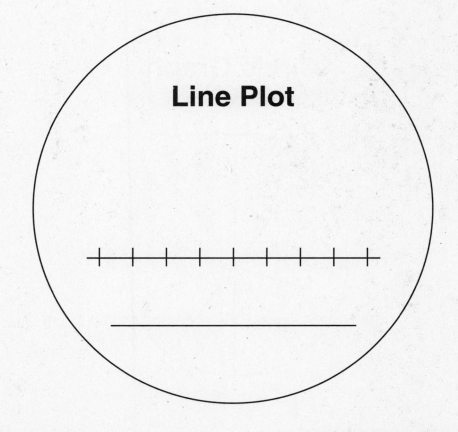

0 1 2 3 4 5 6 7 8

Number of Brothers and Sisters

Line Plot

Gold Medal Graphing

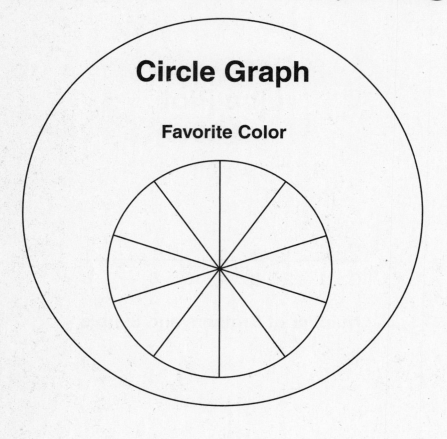

Circle Graph

Favorite Color

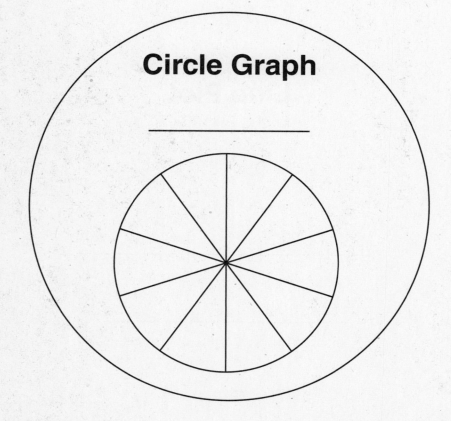

Circle Graph

_____

© Harcourt

Gold Medal Graphing

Bar Graph

Line Graph

© Harcourt

Math First-Aid Kit

Math First-Aid Kit

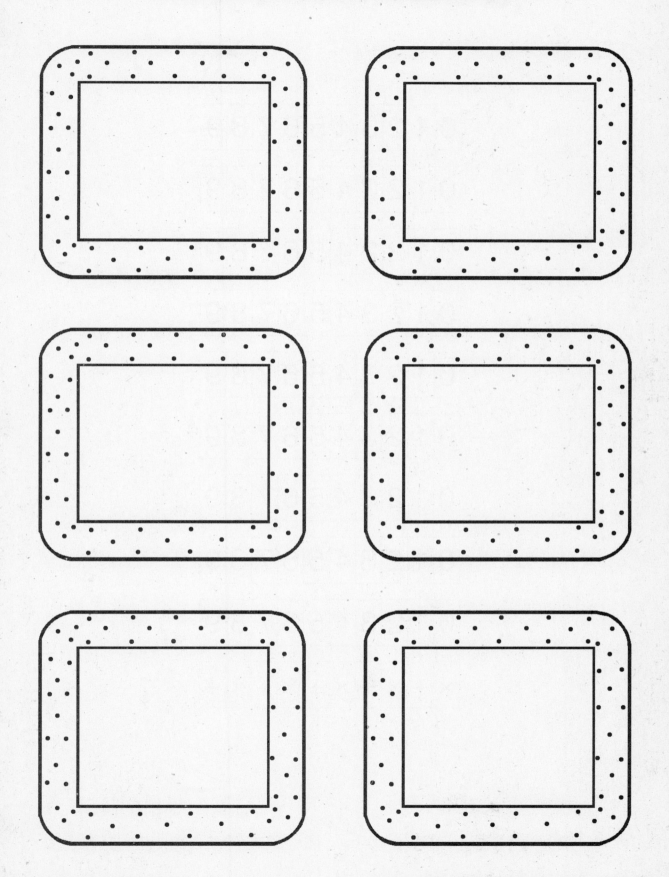

Magnetic Multiplication

0	1	2	3	4	5	6	7	8	9

0	1	2	3	4	5	6	7	8	9

0	1	2	3	4	5	6	7	8	9

0	1	2	3	4	5	6	7	8	9

0	1	2	3	4	5	6	7	8	9

0	1	2	3	4	5	6	7	8	9

0	1	2	3	4	5	6	7	8	9

0	1	2	3	4	5	6	7	8	9

0	1	2	3	4	5	6	7	8	9

×	+	×	+	×	+	×	+	×	+

Fraction Pizza Plates

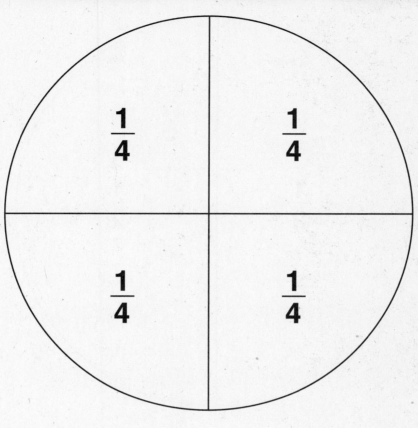

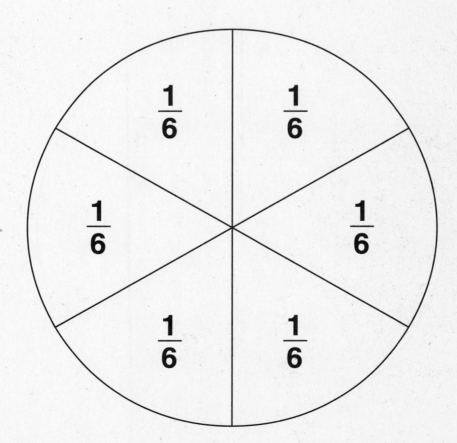

Fraction Pizza Plates

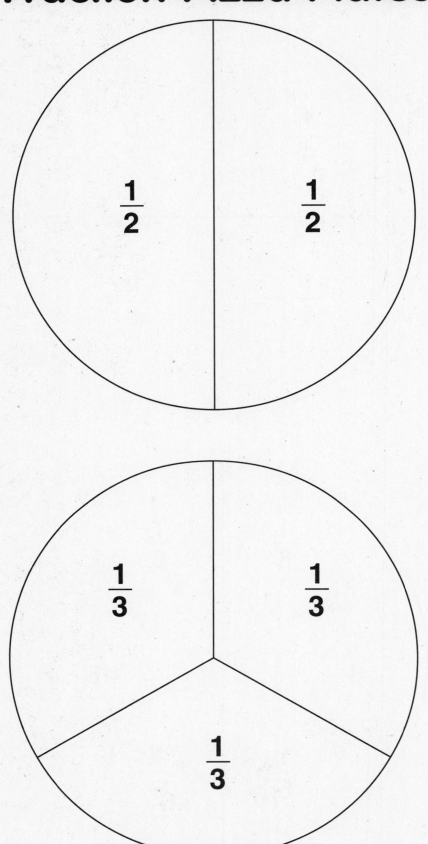

Fraction Pizza Plates

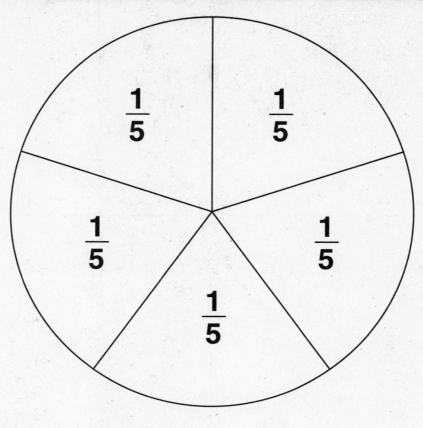

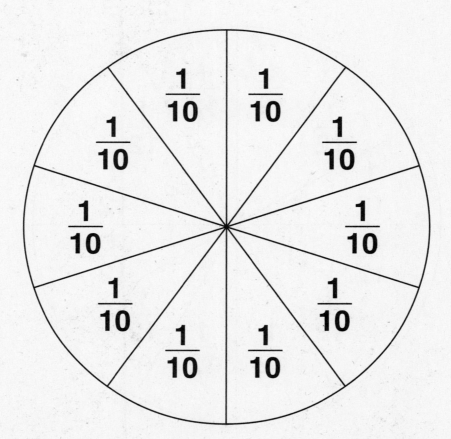

Fraction Pizza Plates

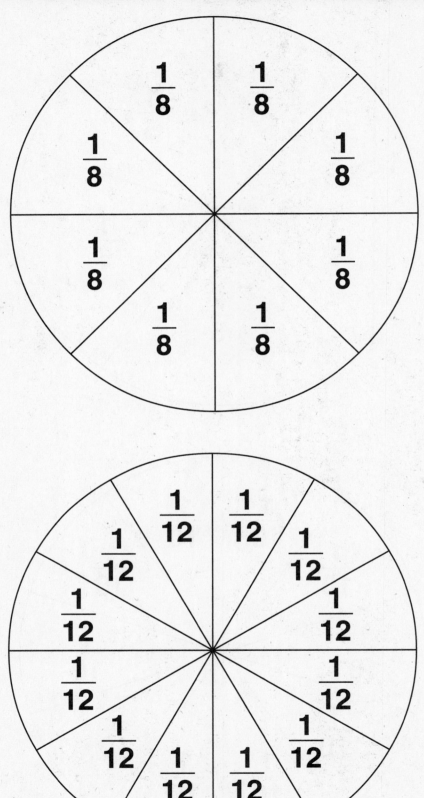